T0357004

Best Easy Day Hikes
Bend and Central Oregon

Help Us Keep This Guide Up to Date

The author and editors have made every effort to make this guide as accurate and useful as possible. However, many things can change after a guide is published—regulations change, facilities come under new management, and so forth.

We would love to hear from you concerning your experiences with this guide and how you feel it could be improved and kept up to date. While we may not be able to respond to all comments and suggestions, we'll take them to heart, and we'll also make certain to share them with the author. Please send your comments and suggestions to 64 S. Main St., Essex, CT 06426.

Thanks for your input!

Best Easy Day Hikes Series

Best Easy Day Hikes
Bend and Central Oregon

Fourth Edition

Lizann Dunegan

ESSEX, CONNECTICUT

FALCONGUIDES®

An imprint of The Globe Pequot Publishing Group, Inc.
64 South Main Street
Essex, CT 06426
www.globepequot.com

Falcon and FalconGuides are registered trademarks and Make Adventure Your Story is a trademark of The Globe Pequot Publishing Group, Inc.

Distributed by NATIONAL BOOK NETWORK

Copyright © 2025 The Globe Pequot Publishing Group, Inc.
Maps by The Globe Pequot Publishing Group, Inc.

British Library Cataloguing-in-Publication Information Available

Library of Congress Cataloging-in-Publication Data Available

ISBN 978-1-4930-8021-2 (paper: alk. paper)
ISBN 978-1-4930-8022-9 (electronic)

∞™ The paper used in this publication meets the minimum requirements of American National Standard for Information Sciences—Permanence of Paper for Printed Library Materials, ANSI/NISO Z39.48-1992.

The author and The Globe Pequot Publishing Group, Inc., assume no liability for accidents happening to, or injuries sustained by, readers who engage in the activities described in this book.

Contents

Redmond

Madras

Prineville

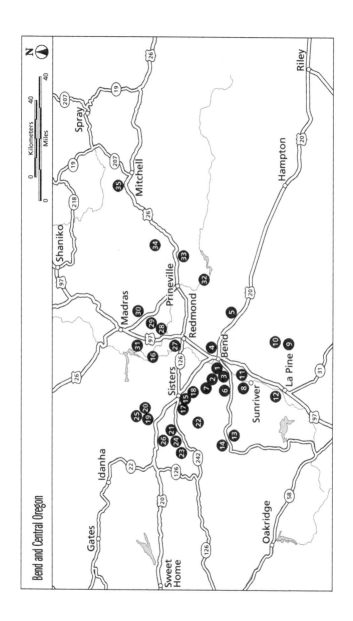

Bend and Central Oregon

Acknowledgments

This hiking guide has always been one of my favorites to update. I want to thank all of my hiking partners and my two canine companions Zane and Zepplin for always wanting to go exploring with me. Also thanks to the Falcon editing team.

Introduction

This small pocket guide contains thirty-five easy day hikes that allow you to explore Bend and surrounding natural areas in Central Oregon. A high-desert ecosystem of sagebrush, juniper, and ponderosa pine characterizes the dry central part of this state, where volcanic activity and erosion have formed amazing gorges and unique rock formations.

Coursing through all of this is the mighty Deschutes River, beginning high in the Cascade Mountains and traveling north to south through the heart of Bend, Central Oregon's largest city.

Many consider Bend the gateway to the High Cascade Lakes Region and Deschutes National Forest. It serves as the geographic and popular center to this area of the state. Many hikes off the Cascade Lakes Highway promise wonderful mountain and lake views, such as the Green Lakes Trail, and the Ray Atkeson Memorial Trail. If you're looking for trails in town, check out the Pilot Butte State Park, Shevlin Park, First Street Rapids Park–Deschutes River Trail, South Deschutes River Trail Loop, and the Old Mill District–Deschutes River Loop.

Afterward, consider visiting the Newberry National Volcanic Monument, which can be easily accessed from the city of Bend (it's southeast of Bend off US 97). Home to Newberry Caldera, a 500-square-mile crater that houses Paulina and East Lakes, this national monument has a rich geologic history, evident in its hot springs, lava flows, and cinder cones. The 0.7-mile Big Obsidian Flow Trail takes you on a fascinating tour of Oregon's youngest lava flow. To see the national monument from a different perspective, try the Paulina Lake Loop, which circles scenic Paulina Lake.

Located northwest of Bend, the small western town of Sisters is a major access point to both the Mount Washington and Mount Jefferson Wilderness Areas—serious volcano country. Trails not to be missed here are Matthieu Lakes, Hand Lake, and Little Belknap Crater. The Matthieu Lakes Loop Trail takes you past two scenic high-alpine lakes and offers nice views of the Central Cascade Mountains. Hand Lake Trail takes you along the shores of scenic Hand Lake and offers stunning views of Mount Washington. Little Belknap Crater Trail takes you across the moonlike landscape of an ancient lava flow. From the summit of the crater, you can enjoy sweeping views of the snow-topped Three Sisters Mountains, Mount Washington, and the surrounding lava flows and craters that make up the Mount Washington Wilderness. For a pristine river hike, take a tour on the West Metolius River Trail and admire the lush, spring-fed river ecosystem. If you enjoy waterfalls, check out the Chush Falls hike. If you don't have much time and you are looking for trails that are close to town, check out the Eagle Rock Loop Trail and the Whychus Creek Trail.

Located 5 miles northeast of Redmond, Smith Rock State Park is also located in the center of this open, high-desert country. It features spectacular pinnacles, columns, and cathedral-like cliffs that rise more than 400 feet above a mammoth gorge carved by the Crooked River. If you are looking for solitude, explore the Gray Butte and Rimrock Springs Natural Area hikes. Both are located within a 30-minute drive of Redmond in the Crooked River National Grasslands and feature high-desert scenery. If you are a fan of hiking along rivers, check out Alder Springs. Located in the Crooked River National Grassland, this hike starts out on a high sagebrush plateau and then drops down into a river canyon. The route follows spring-fed Whychus Creek to where it joins the Deschutes River.

Around Prineville, try the Chimney Rock hike, which promises solitude and nice views of the Crooked River Canyon and distant Central Cascade peaks. A less frequently visited but no less stunning area is the Mill Creek Wilderness, located about 20 miles northeast of Prineville off US 26. Twin Pillars Trail takes you through this wilderness, characterized by open, parklike stands of ponderosa pine, grand fir, and Douglas fir forests. Another destination not to be missed is the Painted Hills Unit of the John Day Fossil Beds National Monument. Several short hikes in this area feature close-up looks at the area's fossil beds and beautifully colored hills.

If you are traveling through Madras, check out the Tam-a-lau Loop Trail that takes you on a tour to the top of a high peninsula above Lake Billy Chinook in Cove Palisades State Park.

Weather

Unlike the Willamette Valley to the west, the central part of the state is generally sunny and dry. The average annual rainfall in this part of the state is 12 inches, and blue skies are the norm. Summer temperatures range from the mid-70s to low 90s; winter temperatures can range from the mid-20s to mid-50s. Be prepared for a substantial amount of snow in the high mountain areas above 4,000 feet and periodic snow showers at lower elevations. Trails at elevations above 4,000 feet may not be accessible until late June into early July.

Preparing for Your Hike

Planning your hiking adventure begins with letting a friend or relative know your trip itinerary so that they can call for help if you don't return at your scheduled time. Your next task is to make sure you are outfitted to experience the risks and rewards of the trail. This section highlights clothing and gear that can help you get the most out of your day hike.

Clothing

Clothing is your armor against Mother Nature's little surprises. Clothing that can be worn in layers is a good strategy for dealing with the often-unpredictable Central Oregon weather. In spring, fall, and winter, the first layer you'll want to wear is a wicking layer of long underwear that keeps perspiration away from your skin. Long underwear made from synthetic fibers is an excellent choice. These fabrics wick moisture away from the skin and draw it to the next layer of clothing, where it then evaporates. Avoid long underwear made of cotton; it is slow to dry and keeps moisture next to your skin.

Your second layer should be an insulating layer. In addition to keeping you warm, this layer needs to "breathe" so that you stay dry while hiking. Two fabrics that provide insulation and dry quickly are fleece and merino wool; a zip-up jacket made of either of these materials is highly recommended.

The last line of layering defense is the shell layer—some type of waterproof, windproof, breathable jacket that'll fit over all your other layers. It should have a large hood that fits over a hat. You'll also need a good pair of rain pants made from a similar waterproof, breathable fabric.

Now that you've learned the basics of layering, don't forget to protect your hands and face. In cold, windy, or rainy weather, you'll need a hat made of wool or fleece. Insulated, waterproof gloves will keep your hands warm and toasty. They'll allow you to remove your outer gloves for close work without exposing the skin.

During the warm summer months, you'll want to wear a wide-brimmed hat, sunglasses, and sunscreen. If you're hiking in spring or summer on a trail next to a lake, creek, or river, be sure to carry mosquito repellent in your pack.

Shoes and Socks

Lightweight hiking boots or trail running shoes are an excellent choice for day hiking. If you'll be hiking in wet weather often, boots or shoes with a Gore-Tex liner will help keep your feet dry.

Socks are another important consideration. Steer clear of cotton socks in favor of socks made of wool or a synthetic blend. These socks provide better cushioning, wick moisture away from your feet, and help prevent blisters.

It's a good idea to bring an extra pair of sandals or an old pair of tennis shoes along if you plan on wading in creeks or swimming in rivers.

Once you've purchased your footwear, be sure to break them in before you hit the trail. New footwear is often stiff and needs to be stretched and molded to your foot for optimum comfort.

Backpacks

A day pack to carry basic trail essentials will help make your day hike more enjoyable. A day pack should have some of the following characteristics: a padded hip belt that's at least 2 inches wide (avoid packs with only a small piece of nylon webbing for a hip belt); a chest strap (which helps stabilize the pack against your body); external pockets to carry water and other items that you want easy access to; an internal pocket to hold keys, a knife, a wallet, and other miscellaneous items; an external lashing system to hold a jacket or windbreaker; and a pocket for carrying a hydration system (a water bladder with an attachable drinking hose). Some hikers like to use a fanny pack to store just a camera, food, a compass, a map, and other trail essentials. Many fanny packs have pockets for two water bottles and a padded hip belt.

Day Hiking Checklist

- day pack
- water and water bottles/water hydration system
- food; high-energy snacks
- first aid kit
- GPS unit
- sunscreen and sunglasses
- matches in waterproof container and fire starter
- insulating top and bottom layers (fleece, wool, etc.)
- rain gear
- winter hat and gloves
- wide-brimmed sun hat, sunscreen, and sunglasses
- insect repellent
- backpacker's trowel, toilet paper, and resealable plastic bags
- camera/film
- cell phone with hiking app
- guidebook
- watch

Trail Regulations/Restrictions

Trails in this guide are located in city parks, state parks, national scenic areas, national forests, and Bureau of Land Management (BLM) lands. Trails located in city parks in this guide do not require special permits or charge use fees. Trailhead fees at some national forest and national scenic area trailheads require a Northwest Forest Pass. You can buy a day pass or an annual pass. For participating national forests and locations for purchasing a Northwest Forest Pass, call (800) 270-7504 or go online to https://store.usgs.gov/forest-pass. A majority of Oregon's state parks require a paid day-use permit, or you can purchase an annual state park permit. You can purchase passes at self-pay machines located at state park trailheads and visitor centers. To purchase an annual state park pass, call (800) 551-6949 (credit card orders only) or visit https://store.oregonstateparks.org/.

Trail Contacts

Hikes 2 and 3: Bend Metro Park & Recreation District, 799 SW Columbia Street, Bend, OR 97702; (541) 389-7275; www.bendparksandrec.org.

Hikes 4, 28, and 31: Oregon Parks and Recreation Department State Parks, 725 Summer Street NE, Suite C, Salem, OR 97301; (503) 986-0707; stateparks.oregon.gov/.

Hikes 5, 27, 29, 30, and 32: Bureau of Land Management, Prineville District Office, 3050 Northeast Third Street, Prineville, OR 97754; (541) 416-6700; www.blm.gov/office/prineville-district-office.

Hikes 7–14: Deschutes National Forest, 63095 Deschutes Market Road, OR 97701; (541) 383-5300; www.fs.usda.gov/recarea/deschutes.

Hikes 15–26: Deschutes National Forest, Sisters Ranger District, 201 N. Pine Street, Sisters, OR 97759; (541) 549-7700; www.fs.usda.gov/recarea/deschutes.

Hikes 33 and 34: Ochoco National Forest, 3160 Northeast Third Street, Prineville, OR 97754; (541) 416-6500; www.fs.usda.gov/ochoco.

Hike 35: John Day Fossil Beds National Monument, 32651 Highway 19, Kimberly, OR 97848; (541) 987-2333; www.nps.gov/joda/planyourvisit/ptd-hills-unit.htm.

Zero Impact

The trails in Central Oregon are quite popular and sometimes can take a beating. We, as trail users and advocates, must be especially vigilant to make sure our passing leaves no lasting mark.

These trails can accommodate plenty of human travel if everyone treats them with respect. Just a few thoughtless or uninformed visitors can ruin the trails for everyone who follows. The book *Leave No Trace* is a valuable resource for learning more about these principles.

Three Falcon Zero-Impact Principles:

- Leave with everything you brought.
- Leave no sign of your visit.
- Leave the landscape as you found it.

Be sure you leave nothing behind, regardless of how small it is. Pack out all your own trash, including biodegradable items like orange peels, which might be sought out by area critters. Also consider picking up any trash that others have left behind.

Follow the main trail. Avoid cutting switchbacks and walking on vegetation beside the trail. Select durable surfaces, such as rocks, logs, or sandy areas, for resting spots.

Don't pick up souvenirs, such as rocks, arrowheads, feathers, or wildflowers. Removing these items will take away from the next hiker's experience.

Avoid making loud noises that may disturb others. Remember, sound travels easily along ridges and through canyons.

Finally, abide by the golden rule of backcountry travel: If you pack it in, pack it out! Thousands of persons coming after you will be thankful for your courtesy.

Map Legend

═══⟨90⟩═══	Interstate Highway
═══⟨97⟩═══	US Highway
═══⟨22⟩═══	State Highway
═══⟨41⟩═══	Local/Forest Roads
═ ═ ═ ═ ═	Unimproved Road
-------	Trail
━━━━━━━	Featured Route
⊢—⊢—⊢	Railroad Grade
Lane Co. / Linn Co.	County Line
	Lava
[⌐ ⌐]	Wilderness/State Forest/Park
[⌐ ⌐]	National Forest/National Park
≍	Bridge
▲	Campground
⯊	Gate
❷	Information
🅟	Parking
≍	Pass
▲	Peak
⛱	Picnic Area
■	Point of Interest/Other Trailhead
🚻	Restroom
⟟	Spring
≣	Steps
❶	Trailhead
⛰	Viewpoint
⅋	Waterfall

Bend

1 First Street Rapids Park–Deschutes River Trail

This easy route, located in downtown Bend, rambles along a scenic section of the Deschutes River. The trail begins at First Street Rapids Park and heads north along the river's edge. After about a mile you'll parallel a golf course as the trail winds through a mix of juniper, sage, and yellow-barked ponderosa pine trees. The last half of the trail winds high on the canyon rim and affords stunning views of Mount Washington and Black Butte to the northwest and the Deschutes River far below. There are also options for side trips that you can take on the Upper Sawyer Canyon Trail and the Archie Briggs Canyon Trail.

Distance: 7.8 miles out and back

Hiking time: 2.5-4 hours

Elevation gain: 120 feet

Trail surface: Dirt path, wood chip trail

Best season: Open year-round. Snow may be present during the winter months.

Other trail users: Runners and mountain bikers

Canine compatibility: Leashed dogs permitted

Fees and permits: No fees or permits required

Schedule: Open 5 a.m. to 10 p.m.

Maps: Bend Urban Trails

USGS map: Bend, OR

Finding the Trailhead: From Bend Parkway north in Bend, take exit 137 for Revere Avenue/Downtown Bend. At the end of the off-ramp, turn left onto Revere Avenue and go 0.1 mile. Turn left onto Wall Street. Continue 0.2 mile and turn right onto Portland Avenue. Continue 0.2 mile on Portland Avenue and turn right onto First Street.

Continue 0.3 mile to where the street dead-ends at First Street Rapids Park. GPS: N44 20.934' / W120 20.934'

The Hike

First Street Rapids Park is the starting point for this fun route that follows a graded path along the Deschutes River through downtown Bend. This park is a popular put-in spot for kayakers, and you will often see paddlers playing in the water. Watch for small groups of ducks, blue herons, and Canada geese feeding along the riverbank. At 0.7 mile you'll cross Mount Washington Drive and continue on the smooth grade of the well-groomed trail as it continues north. At this point the trail parallels the greens of the River's Edge Golf Course before it enters a forest corridor that passes through several residential areas. After 1.3 miles you will pass the Upper Sawyer Canyon Trail on the left, which leads to Sawyer Uplands Park. Continue a short distance and then arrive at Robert S. Sawyer Park. This park covers over 42 acres and is popular for bird watching. You can cross the Deschutes River on a wooden footbridge if you want to explore the other side of the river. There is also a portable restroom located at this park. Over the next 2.6 miles you'll cross two more paved roads as the path winds through an area of expensive homes high above the river. At 2.8 miles you have another opportunity for a side trip to explore the Archie Briggs Canyon Trail. For this hike continue on the Deschutes River Trail. Along this section of the trail, you can see the snowcapped peaks of Mount Washington, Black Butte, and other Central Cascade peaks that dominate the skyline to the west. At 3.9 miles the Deschutes River Trail ends at a green gate where you will turn around and retrace the route back to the trailhead.

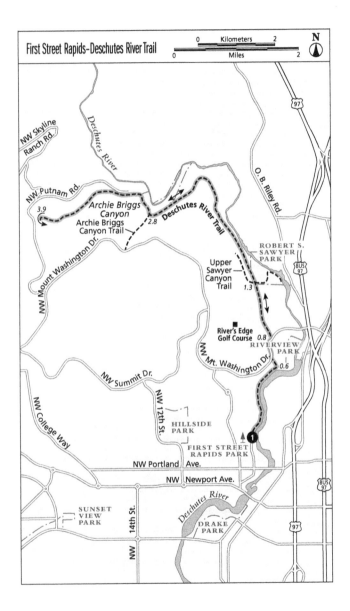

First Street Rapids–Deschutes River Trail

Kilometers 0 — 2
Miles 0 — 2

N

NW Skyline Ranch Rd.

Deschutes River

NW 97

NW Putnam Rd.

3.9

Archie Briggs Canyon

Archie Briggs Canyon Trail

2.8

Deschutes River Trail

O. B. Riley Rd.

ROBERT S. SAWYER PARK

BUS 97

NW Mount Washington Dr.

Upper Sawyer Canyon Trail

1.3

River's Edge Golf Course

0.8

RIVERVIEW PARK

NW Mt. Washington Dr.

0.6

NW Summit Dr.

NW College Way

NW 12th St.

HILLSIDE PARK

FIRST STREET RAPIDS PARK

1

NW Portland Ave.

NW Newport Ave.

BUS 97

SUNSET VIEW PARK

14th St.

NW

Deschutes River

DRAKE PARK

97

Miles and Directions

0.0 From First Street Rapids Park, begin hiking north on the well-graded trail that parallels the scenic Deschutes River. A portable restroom is available at the trailhead.

0.6 Turn left onto the graded trail (don't go right toward the golf course).

0.7 The trail intersects with the paved Mount Washington Drive. Turn right and follow the trail downhill as it parallels Mount Washington Drive. Look for the small DESCHUTES RIVER TRAIL signs marking the trail.

0.8 Turn left and cross Mount Washington Drive. Pick up the trail on the other side. Continue on the sidewalk for 0.1 mile.

0.9 Turn left and continue on the graded path.

1.3 Pass the Upper Sawyer Canyon Trail on the left. Continue on the main trail a short distance and then arrive at a trail junction with the signed ROBERT S. SAWYER PARK TRAIL. Stay to the left and continue on the Deschutes River Trail.

2.0 Cross Archie Briggs Road and continue on the graded trail on the other side.

2.3 Go around a green metal gate.

2.8 The Archie Briggs Canyon Trail goes left. Continue straight on the Deschutes River Trail.

3.9 The Deschutes River Trail ends at a green gate. Turn around and follow the same route back to the trailhead.

7.8 Arrive back at the trailhead.

2 Old Mill District–Deschutes River Loop

This scenic river hike takes you along the banks of the Deschutes River in the Old Mill District—a popular shopping area in Bend. The route starts in Farewell Bend Park and completes a loop past several viewpoints of the river where you'll see mallard ducks, Canada geese, and blue herons. If you are hiking with your dog, you will also have an opportunity to visit the leash-free Riverbend Dog Park. This area has many other hiking options if you are looking for a longer or shorter hike.

Distance: 2.7-mile loop
Hiking time: 1–2 hours
Elevation gain: 100 feet
Trail surface: Paved path and dirt path
Best season: Open year-round
Other trail users: Runners and cyclists

Canine compatibility: Leashed dogs permitted
Fees and permits: No fees or permits required
Schedule: Open 5 a.m. to 10 p.m.
Maps: Bend Urban Trails
USGS map: Bend, OR

Finding the trailhead: From Bend Parkway on the south side of Bend, take exit 139 for Reed Market Road/Old Mill District. At the end of the off-ramp, turn right onto Reed Market Road. Continue 0.5 mile on Reed Market Road and turn right into the Farewell Bend Park parking area. GPS: N44 02.451' / W121 19.241'

Old Mill District—Deschutes River Loop

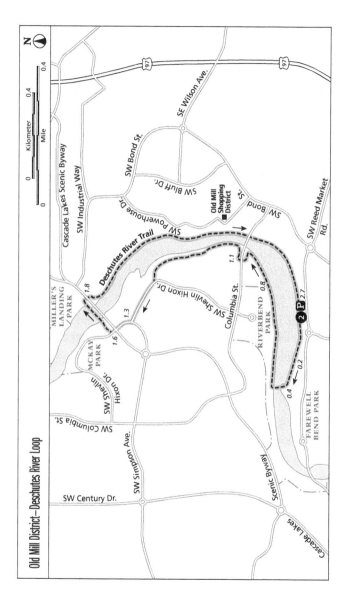

The Hike

This scenic urban loop hike takes you along the banks of the Deschutes River in the Old Mill District neighborhood and shopping area in Southwest Bend. The Old Mill District is a fun shopping center that features a movie theater, retail shops, and many restaurants. If you need to pick up any hiking gear, REI has a large store located in this shopping district.

The hike starts at Farewell Bend Park adjacent to the Deschutes River. Farewell Bend Park covers 22 acres and features a natural marsh and canoe launch. It also features a wildlife viewing ramp to explore at the 0.2-mile mark. It takes you out onto the Deschutes River where you may see mallard ducks, Canada geese and other birdlife. After 0.4 mile you will cross the Deschutes River and head north.

The Deschutes River flows wide and slow along this section and is very popular for canoeing, kayaking, and stand-up paddleboarding. After another 0.4 mile you will pass Riverbend Park. This 13.9-acre park provides access to the Deschutes River, has large grassy areas and public restrooms, and also features a fenced, leash-free dog park. If you are interested in exploring the shops and restaurants in the Old Mill District shopping area, you can cross the bridge at 1.1 miles and take a tour of this popular shopping district. After 1.6 miles cross the Deschutes River on a footbridge and complete the return loop as the path continues along the river's edge.

Miles and Directions

0.0 From the parking area, turn left (south) and walk on the paved path.

0.2 Turn right and start walking on a ramp that takes you out to a viewpoint on the river. After enjoying the views, walk back to the main paved path and turn right.

0.4 Turn right and cross a bridge. After crossing the bridge turn right (north). (*Option*: If you are looking for a longer hike, you can turn left and continue on south on the Deschutes River Trail.)

0.8 Pass the Riverbend leash-free dog park on the left.

1.0 Turn right and walk through a short tunnel. After going through the tunnel, stay to the right.

1.1 Pass a bridge on your right. You have the option of turning right and going over the bridge to explore the Old Mill District shops. Continue straight on the paved path.

1.3 Turn right and continue walking on the sidewalk.

1.5 Turn right and onto the Southwest Shevlin Hixon Road and continue walking on the sidewalk.

1.6 Walk under a bridge and turn right onto the paved path and cross the river on the footbridge.

1.8 After crossing the footbridge, continue straight. Cross Southwest Industrial Way and then continue on the paved path.

2.4 Walk through a tunnel.

2.7 Arrive back at the trailhead.

3 South Deschutes River Loop

This beautiful loop takes you along both side of the scenic Deschutes River on the popular Deschutes River Trail in the south part of Bend. There are several great swimming opportunities, and the route also travels through Farewell Bend Park, which has restrooms, water, and picnic tables.

Distance: 5.8-mile loop
Hiking time: 2.5-4 hours
Elevation gain: 230 feet
Trail surface: Dirt path, paved path
Best season: Open year-round. Snow may be present during the winter months.

Other trail users: Runners
Canine compatibility: Leashed dogs permitted
Fees and permits: No fees or permits required
Schedule: Open dawn to 10 p.m.
Maps: Bend Urban Trails
USGS map: Bend, OR

Finding the trailhead: In Bend, drive south on Bond Street for 1.7 miles to the intersection with Brookswood Boulevard. Continue driving through three roundabouts and turn right onto Sweetbriar Way. Turn left onto Snowbrush Drive and then turn right onto Pine Drive and park at River Canyon Park. GPS: N44 0.56' / W121 21.10'

The Hike

This fun urban hike starts in River Canyon Park and follows a gravel road along a large irrigation pipe managed by the Central Oregon Irrigation District (COID) for a little over a mile of the route. The district provides water for about 45,000 acres in Central Oregon. More than 700 miles of canals provide agricultural and industrial water to the Terrebonne, Redmond, Bend, Alfalfa, and Powell Butte areas.

After you turn onto the signed DESCHUTES RIVER TRAIL you'll cross the rumbling Deschutes River on the Conley Brooks Bridge. Viewing the river from the bridge gives you a different perspective as the whitewater of this dynamic river rushes down the canyon. After crossing the bridge you'll continue to follow the Deschutes River Trail as it winds through a predominantly ponderosa pine forest dotted with manzanita. At different points along this trail you'll also see the holly-like dark green leaves of the Oregon Grape (the Oregon state flower). The Oregon Grape produces clusters of edible blue berries during the summer months. Native people ate the berries and also used the roots of this plant to make yellow dye. At your halfway point, you'll cross the river and then follow the Deschutes River Trail as it heads back upriver traveling through Farewell Bend Park. This park has a shady pavilion with picnic tables, restrooms, and water and provides easy river access and good swimming opportunities.

At 3.8 miles you'll pass a hydropower plant that is carefully camouflaged with foliage. The source water that turns the turbines comes from a preexisting diversion site a little over a mile upstream. The water flows 135 feet downhill through a buried pipe to the turbines. The electricity that is produced joins the power grid and the profit from the electricity generated is used to fund water conservation projects that are managed by the COID. As you continue on the return loop the trail winds through more ponderosa pine forest and offers many nice views of the Deschutes River. The last 1.2 miles of the route you'll join up with the COID gravel road that takes you back to your starting point.

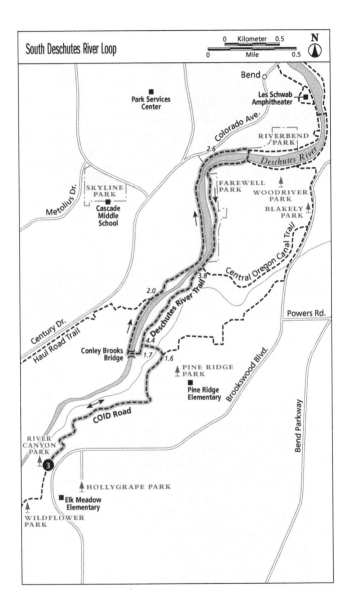

Miles and Directions

0.0 Start walking on the paved path. You will pass some picnic tables and a viewpoint.

0.1 At the end of the path, turn right onto the COID gravel road and walk toward the river and around a green gate.

0.3 The road comes to a T junction. Stay to the right. Cross over an irrigation bridge over an irrigation canal.

0.5 Pass a viewing platform on the left.

1.4 Turn left onto a gravel path (the COID road heads up the hill). Continue descending on the gravel path until you reach the signed DESCHUTES RIVER TRAIL.

1.6 Turn left and follow the trail upriver.

1.7 Cross Conley Brooks Bridge over the river. After crossing the bridge, turn right and continue on the dirt trail.

2.0 Stay right at the trail junction (the route that goes left is the Haul Road Trail).

2.6 Proceed through the opening in the black metal fence and continue straight on the Deschutes River Trail. Cross the river over a bridge. Stay to the right and arrive at Farewell Bend Park, which has water and restrooms. Continue following the Deschutes River Trail on the return loop upriver.

3.8 Walk on a wooden boardwalk and then pass a power plant. At the next trail intersection, keep straight (right). The signed trail that goes left is the signed CENTRAL OREGON CANAL TRAIL.

4.0 At the trail junction go right.

4.4 Take a sharp left and head uphill.

4.6 Turn right on the COID gravel road.

5.8 Arrive back at the trailhead.

4 Pilot Butte State Park

This popular urban hike takes you to the summit of Pilot Butte—a prominent cinder cone and landmark in downtown Bend. You will follow the scenic Bob Bristol Nature Trail 480 feet to the summit where you'll have fantastic views of Mount Bachelor, the Three Sisters, Broken Top, Black Butte, and many other Cascade peaks. There are additional trail options in this park. You can follow the Base Trail, which is a mile-long trail that circles the base of Pilot Butte, and you also have the option of hiking 3.4 miles out and back on the Larkspur Trail, which takes you to the Bend Senior Center and Larkspur Park. You can also follow an alternate summit trail that parallels the paved road to the summit or walk on the jogging track in the park.

Distance: 1.8 miles out and back
Hiking time: 1–1.5 hours
Elevation gain: 480 feet
Trail surface: Paved path and dirt path
Best season: Open year-round. Snow may be present during the winter months.

Other trail users: Runners
Canine compatibility: Leashed dogs permitted
Fees and permits: No fees or permits required
Schedule: Open dawn to dusk
Maps: Bend Urban Trail System map
USGS map: Pilot Butte, OR

Finding the trailhead: From Northeast Third Street/US 97 (Business) in Bend, turn east onto Greenwood Avenue/US 20. Continue 1.4 miles and turn left onto Northeast Azure Drive at the second PILOT BUTTE TRAILHEAD sign. Follow signs for another 0.3 mile to a large parking area and trailhead. GPS: N44 03.469' / W121 16.706'

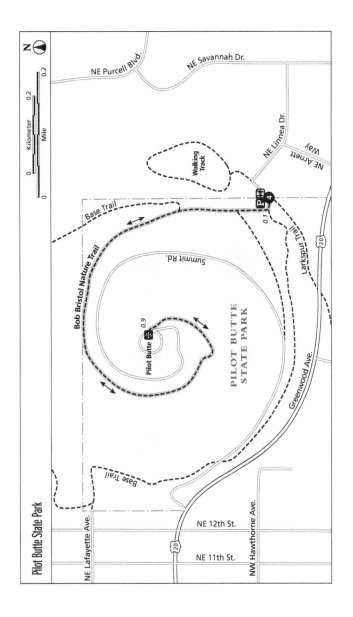

The Hike

Pilot Butte has a small system of trails that will satisfy all types of hikers. This hike takes you on the Bob Bristol Nature Trail, which winds 480 feet to the summit of Pilot Butte. Pilot Butte is an extinct cinder cone and is a well-known Central Oregon landmark. The first European settlers in this area called the formation "Red Butte" due to its reddish-colored soil.

This route starts at the base of the butte where you will find restrooms with water, picnic tables, and a walking track. Follow the well-graded trail as it winds around the butte at a steep pace. The trail is shaded in spots by native western juniper, which is the most common tree that grows on the butte. Sagebrush, bluebunch wheatgrass, and Idaho fescue can also be seen along the trail. In the spring, you may see wildflowers blooming, including rock cress, yarrow, bright red paintbrush, purple lupine, penstemon, and mariposa lily. Rest benches and interpretive signs are interspersed along the trail if you want to take a break. Once you arrive at the summit you can enjoy a 360-degree view of downtown Bend and Mount Bachelor, the Three Sisters, Broken Top, and other Central Cascade peaks. After you soak in the views, retrace the route back to the parking area.

Miles and Directions

0.0 Start hiking on the paved path accessed from the south end of the main parking area. (See Options for other trails in the park that begin from this paved parking area.)

0.1 Turn right onto the signed BOB BRISTOL NATURE TRAIL, which climbs to the 4,138-foot summit of Pilot Butte.

0.9 Arrive at the paved summit road. Continue straight, then cross the summit road and walk up the steps to the summit viewpoint. After soaking in the views, retrace your footsteps down Pilot Butte.

1.8 Arrive back at the trailhead.

Options: Pilot Butte State Park has other trail options. If you don't feel like hiking to the summit, you can follow the mile-long Base Trail, circling the base of the butte. If you are looking for a longer hike, you can follow the paved Larkspur Trail, which takes you 1.7 miles one way to the Bend Senior Center and Larkspur Park.

5 Flatiron Rock-Ancient Juniper Trail

This route explores the Flatiron Trail and the Ancient Juniper Trail in the Oregon Badlands Wilderness. The hike takes you through a high desert landscape of old-growth juniper to the summit of Flatiron Rock where you'll enjoy spectacular views of the Central Oregon Cascades. After soaking in the views, you return on the Flatiron Trail to the turnoff to the Ancient Juniper Trail, where you complete a loop through more spectacular old-growth juniper.

Distance: 6.6-mile figure eight
Hiking time: 2.5-3.5 hours
Elevation gain: 100 feet
Trail surface: Dirt and sand trail
Best season: Sept through May. This trail is very hot during the summer months.
Other trail users: Runners
Canine compatibility: Leashed dogs permitted. This trail is not a good option for dogs during July and Aug due to extreme heat.
Fees and permits: No fees or permits required
Schedule: Open all hours
Maps: BLM Oregon Badlands Wilderness Trails
USGS map: Horse Ridge, OR

Finding the trailhead: From the intersection of US 97 (Business) and US 20, travel 15.8 miles east of downtown Bend on US 20. Turn left into the signed FLATIRON ROCK TRAILHEAD. GPS: N43 57.46' / W121 3.115'

The Hike

The Oregon Badlands Wilderness is a unique wilderness habitat that covers almost 30,000 acres and has over 50 miles of trails to explore. Local citizens rallied and supported

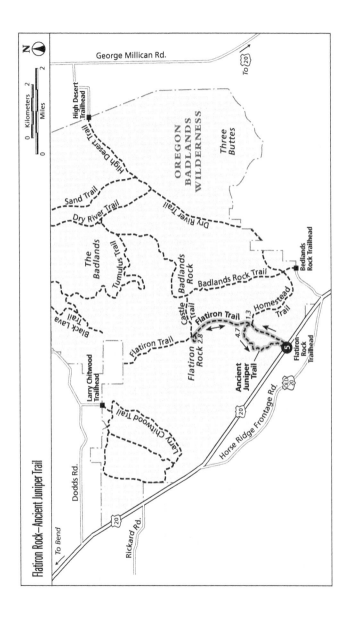

Flatiron Rock–Ancient Juniper Trail

Senator Ron Wyden when he introduced the Oregon Badlands Wilderness Act in June 2008, and in March 2009 the Oregon Badlands Wilderness Act was signed into law by President Barack Obama.

This wilderness features a vast, western juniper forest sprinkled with fragrant-smelling sagebrush, rabbitbrush, and bitterbrush and interesting geologic formations. Wildlife that you may see in this wilderness area includes red-tailed hawks, ravens, coyotes, jackrabbits, and quail. This route flanks the edge of the Badlands shield volcano and takes you to the rocky outcropping known as Flatiron Rock. Once you reach this unique rock outcropping, you can explore a short loop trail that gives you a different perspective of this unique rock formation. On the return trip you can loop back to the trailhead on the Ancient Juniper Trail, which circles through more of the ancient juniper forest that is the centerpiece of this high-desert region. This area is very hot and dry in the summer months, and it is a good idea to bring extra water.

Miles and Directions

0.0 Start hiking on the Flatiron Trail, which heads to the right.

1.2 Arrive at the junction with Ancient Juniper Trail. Continue straight (right).

1.3 Arrive at the junction with the Homestead Trail. Continue straight (left).

2.8 Arrive at a three-way trail junction. Turn left and start hiking the trail to the top of Flatiron Rock. (The Flatiron Trail continues straight and the Castle Trail goes right at this junction.) Once you reach the top, enjoy the views and complete a small loop that tours Flatiron Rock. Once you complete the loop, return to the Castle Trail/Flatiron Trail junction.

3.1 Turn right onto the Flatiron Trail.

4.7 Arrive at the junction with the Ancient Juniper Trail and turn right.

6.6 Arrive back at the trailhead.

6 Shevlin Park Loop

This fun hike is a local favorite and is only minutes from downtown Bend. The route winds through ponderosa pine and Douglas fir forest along the banks of picturesque Tumalo Creek in Shevlin Park.

Distance: 5.0-mile loop
Hiking time: 2–3 hours
Elevation gain: 250 feet
Trail surface: Graded gravel path and dirt path
Best season: Open year-round. Snow may be present during the winter months.

Other trail users: Runners and mountain bikers
Canine compatibility: Leashed dogs permitted
Fees and permits: No fees or permits required
Schedule: Open 5 a.m. to 10 p.m.
Maps: Bend Urban Trails Map
USGS map: Bend, OR

Finding the trailhead: From Bend Parkway north in Bend, take exit 137 for Revere Avenue/Downtown Bend. At the end of the off-ramp, turn left onto Revere Avenue and go 0.1 mile. Turn left onto Wall Street. Continue 0.2 mile and turn right onto Portland Avenue. Continue 0.7 mile on Portland Avenue and turn left onto 9th Street. Go one block and turn right onto Newport Avenue. Continue 3.3 miles on Newport Avenue to the Shevlin Park entrance on the left. Drive through the first parking area and continue 0.1 mile to a second parking area that has a vault toilet. GPS: N43 56.356' / W121 24.776'

The Hike

This route explores the 647-acre Shevlin Park, which was donated by the Shevlin-Hixon Company to the city of Bend in 1920. The park features hiking and mountain biking trails; beautiful Tumalo Creek flows through the center of the park.

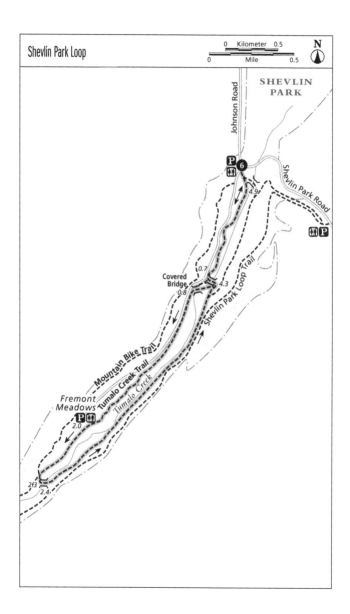

Shevlin Park Loop

This park is also very popular with trail runners, who enjoy running on its well-graded paths. This park is named for the company's president, Thomas H. Shevlin. At one time Shevlin-Hixon operated one of the largest lumber mills in the country. Its first mill in Bend opened in 1916 and began processing what seemed to be an endless supply of trees. Eventually the tree supply was exhausted. In 1950 Shevlin-Hixon Mill was purchased by Brooks Scanlon and closed shortly thereafter.

This picturesque hike leads through shimmering aspen trees and stately ponderosa pine trees along the edge of Tumalo Creek. According to Lewis L. McArthur, the author of *Oregon Geographic Names*, the name Tumalo is possibly derived from the word Temolo, which means "wild plum" in the Klamath tribe language, or the Klamath tribe word Temola, which translates to "ground fog." The path is well graded, and there are many opportunities to stop and admire the creek at one of the many picnic areas scattered along the route. You will cross the creek on footbridges at different points along the way. After 2 miles you'll arrive at historic Fremont Meadows. In 1843, John C. Fremont, an explorer for the US government, and his group camped in this meadow. You also can take a side trip and explore the Shevlin Meadow Interpretive Trail. After 2.4 miles you will cross the creek on the upper foot bridge and then begin ascending a forested ridge. As you hike the ridge you'll have nice views of the creek canyon. Over the next 2.6 miles the trail takes you along the ridge high above the creek and then descends once again into the creek canyon back to your starting point.

Miles and Directions

0.0 Start walking on the paved path by the restrooms that heads toward the creek and picnic structure.

0.1 Continue on the dirt path that travels past the picnic shelter. Once you arrive at the creek, turn right onto the well-graded sand/gravel path.

0.7 Arrive at the signed LARCH GROVE area. Cross a bridge over Tumalo Creek. The trail Ys after crossing the bridge. Go right and continue on the signed CREEK TRAIL. The Shevlin Park Loop Trail goes left.

0.8 Turn right at the trail junction and cross the covered bridge. After crossing the bridge go left and continue on the Creek Trail.

2.0 Arrive at Fremont Meadow. (*Option:* Take a short side trip on the Shevlin Meadow Interpretive Trail, which starts here.) Continue hiking on the Creek Trail.

2.3 Arrive at a three-way junction. Stay to the left toward the signed upper footbridge.

2.4 Cross the footbridge and continue as the trail ascends the ridge.

3.0 Cross a log bridge over a side creek.

3.1 Arrive at a trail junction. Turn left toward the signed SHEVLIN PARK entrance. The Shevlin Park Loop Trail goes right.

3.9 Go left at a T junction. The trail turns into a doubletrack road.

4.1 Turn left toward the Shevlin Park entrance.

4.2 Turn left onto the signed TUMALO CREEK TRAIL and start walking downhill. (The Shevlin Park Loop Trail goes right.)

4.3 Turn right at the trail junction and cross a footbridge over Tumalo Creek.

4.4 The trail intersects with the paved road. Go right and continue hiking on the path.

4.9 Turn left at the trail junction and walk past the picnic shelter.

5.0 Arrive back at the trailhead.

7 Tumalo Falls

This route takes you along scenic Tumalo Creek and has many wonderful views of different waterfalls, including Tumalo Falls, Double Falls, and Upper Falls. There are additional options for a longer hike to Happy Valley.

Distance: 4.4 miles out and back

Hiking time: 2-3 hours

Elevation gain: 700 feet

Trail surface: Graded gravel path and dirt path

Best season: May through Oct. Snow may be present during the winter months.

Other trail users: Runners and mountain bikers (mountain bikers are only allowed to ride uphill on this trail).

Canine compatibility: Leashed dogs permitted

Fees and permits: A Northwest Forest Pass is required. You can purchase a pass online at store. usgs.gov/forest-pass or by calling (800) 270-7504.

Schedule: Open all hours

Maps: Bend Adventure Map

USGS map: Tumalo Falls, OR

Finding the trailhead: From the intersection of Northwest Galveston Avenue and 14th Street in Bend, follow Northwest Galveston (which turns into Northwest Skyliner's Road) for 10 miles. The road Ys and turns to gravel. Turn left onto FR 4603 and follow it for 2.5 miles (the gravel road is wash-boarded in different sections) to the trailhead. GPS: N44 01.927' / W121 33.990'

The Hike

This route takes you on a tour along Tumalo Creek and past a series of picturesque waterfalls. The Tumalo Creek Canyon was carved by glaciers. The source of Tumalo Creek is a

Tumalo Falls

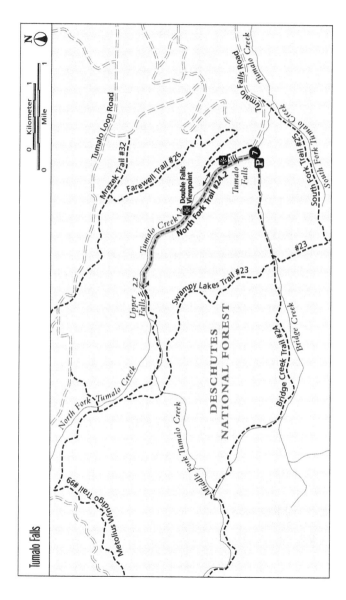

series of springs that ensure consistent water flow year-round. About 46 million gallons of Tumalo Creek water is used to irrigate 8,000 acres of farmland each year. In addition, Bridge Creek (a tributary of Tumalo Creek) provides drinking water for Bend residents.

This route is a very popular hike due to its proximity to Bend and its well-groomed trail with many waterfalls. Because of this, it is recommended that you try this hike on a weekday to avoid the weekend crowds. There are restrooms at the start of this hike and interpretive signs. Start hiking on the signed NORTH FORK TRAIL as it heads uphill for 0.2 mile to a scenic overlook of 97-foot Tumalo Falls. As you continue on the trail, it winds along the creek's edge through a thick forest of mountain hemlock and Engelmann spruce. At the signed viewpoint at 1.2 miles, you'll have a spectacular view of Double Falls, which follows a curvy path to a twin cascade. Continue another mile up the trail to another signed viewpoint of the shimmering cascade of Upper Falls. This is your turnaround point. You have the option to continue on this trail as it passes more spectacular creek scenery until it intersects with the Swampy Lakes Trail in 1.5 miles. If you turn left onto the Swampy Lakes Trail, you can make a loop. If you want to complete a longer out-and-back hike on the same trail (this option has the best scenery), then at the Swampy Lakes Trail Junction stay to the right and hike another 0.7 mile to Happy Valley, where you can view bright splashes of wildflowers in the summer months.

Miles and Directions

0.0 Enjoy a wonderful view of Tumalo Falls from the viewing platform at the trailhead. Start hiking on the signed NORTH FORK TRAIL 24.2 as it heads uphill.

0.2 Arrive at a viewpoint of Tumalo Falls.

1.2 Pass a signed viewpoint of Double Falls on the right.

2.2 Pass a signed viewpoint of the Upper Falls on the right. This is your turnaround point. Retrace the route back to the trailhead.

4.4 Arrive back at the trailhead.

Options: Continue another 2.2 miles to Happy Valley where you'll find beautiful wildflower scenery during the summer months. Travel 1.5 miles to the intersection with the Swampy Lakes Trail, stay to the right, and continue 0.7 mile to Happy Valley. Or, make a loop by traveling 1.5 miles to the intersection with the Swampy Lakes Trail, then turn left and follow the Swampy Lakes Trail for 2.1 miles to the junction with the Bridge Creek Trail. Turn left onto the Bridge Creek Trail and hike 1.3 miles back to the trailhead.

8 Benham Falls–Deschutes River Trail

This route follows the southern segment of the Deschutes River Trail. It takes you through a magnificent old-growth ponderosa pine forest along the banks of the moody Deschutes River. Highlights of the route include a spectacular viewpoint of Benham Falls, grand views of South Sister and Broken Top, and opportunities to see ospreys and other wildlife. Options to hike farther on the Deschutes River Trail are available.

Distance: 2.0 miles out and back (with longer options)
Hiking time: 1–1.5 hours
Elevation gain: 100 feet
Trail surface: Dirt path
Best season: Open year-round. The driest months are May through Oct. Snow may be present during the winter months.
Other trail users: Mountain bikers and trail runners

Canine compatibility: Leashed dogs permitted
Fees and permits: A Northwest Forest Pass is required. You can purchase a pass online at store. usgs.gov/forest-pass or by calling (800) 270-7504.
Schedule: Open all hours
Maps: Deschutes National Forest Map
USGS map: Benham Falls, OR

Finding the trailhead: From the intersection of Northwest Franklin and US 97 (Business) in Bend, travel 11.2 miles south on US 97 to the LAVA LANDS VISITOR CENTER sign. Turn right (west) onto the entrance road and then take an immediate left onto FR 9702, where a sign indicates DESCHUTES RIVER 4/BENHAM FALLS 4. Continue 4 miles to a gravel parking area at Benham Falls Day Use Picnic Area.

    Shuttle directions to Meadow Day Use Area: Head 6.2 miles west of Bend on the Cascade Lakes Highway (OR 46) and turn left onto gravel FR 100 at the MEADOW PICNIC AREA sign. Continue 1.4 miles to the parking area at Benham Falls Day Use Picnic Area. GPS: N43 54.559' / W121 21.452'

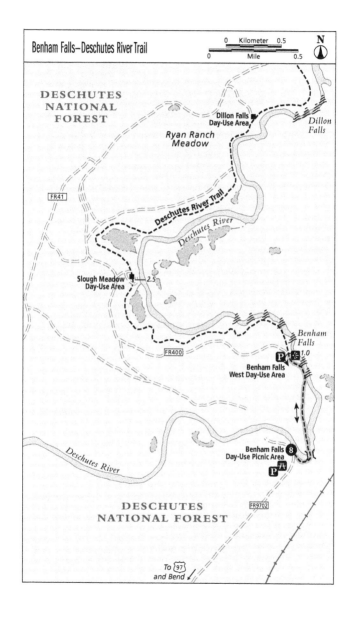

Benham Falls–Deschutes River Trail

0   Kilometer   0.5

0   Mile   0.5

N

DESCHUTES
NATIONAL
FOREST

*Ryan Ranch
Meadow*

Dillon Falls
Day-Use Area

*Dillon
Falls*

FR41

Deschutes River Trail

Deschutes River

Slough Meadow
Day-Use Area
2.5

*Benham
Falls*

FR400

P 1.0

Benham Falls
West Day-Use Area

Deschutes River

Benham Falls
Day-Use Picnic Area 8

P

FR9702

DESCHUTES
NATIONAL
FOREST

To 97
and Bend

The Hike

This route starts at the picturesque Benham Falls Day Use Picnic Area that is set among towering old-growth ponderosa pine trees. The day-use area has picnic tables, fire rings, and restrooms. You'll begin the hike by walking on a forested path along the banks of the Deschutes River. The river is very quiet and wide along this section because of a manmade logjam located above the wooden bridge that crosses the river. This logjam was built in the 1920s to help protect bridge pilings from debris floating down the river. Plants and grass have grown on top of the logs, creating an "almost" natural dam on the river. At 0.1 mile you'll cross the river over a long wooden bridge. Over the next 0.5 mile you'll walk on a wide multiuse path that is popular with mountain bikers. At 0.7 mile you'll turn off the multiuse path onto a hiking trail that follows the contours of the river. As you approach Benham Falls, the character of the river changes from slow and meandering to fast and furious as the river channel narrows. At 0.8 mile you'll arrive at a spectacular viewpoint of Benham Falls. The river roars over jagged lava through a narrow canyon. From here the route continues along the shores of the river, where you'll have views of a magnificent lava flow on the opposite side of the river and spectacular views of South Sister and Broken Top. Ospreys feed and nest along this section of the river. Also known as "fish hawks" they feed on the large stocks of trout present in the river. You can identify ospreys by their predominantly white undersides and black markings on the top of their wings. Their heads are white with a distinctive black band across their eyes and cheeks. Look for their nests, which are usually located in the tops of dead trees. You have the option to hike farther on the Deschutes River Trail. You can hike another 1.5 miles to Slough Meadow Day Use Area, or you can continue another 7.7 miles to the Meadow Picnic Area. If you want to hike one way, you can set up a shuttle by leaving a vehicle at the Meadow Day Use Area. See below for driving directions to the Meadow Day Use Area.

Miles and Directions

Meadow Day Use Area

0.0 Start by hiking on the trail signed DESCHUTES RIVER TRAIL NO. 2.1, which begins at the river's edge opposite the picnic area. Another sign indicates BENHAM FALLS ½, DILLON FALLS 3½, LAVA ISLAND FALLS 7, MEADOW DAY USE 8½.

0.1 Cross a long wooden bridge over the Deschutes River.

0.7 Veer right onto the hiking trail, indicated by a hiker symbol.

0.8 The hiking trail intersects the wide biking trail. Turn right and continue on the narrower hiking trail. Proceed about 200 yards to a T intersection. Turn right and descend to a viewpoint of Benham Falls. (If you go left at this junction, you'll arrive at the Benham Falls West Day Use Area, which has restrooms and picnic tables.)

1.0 Arrive at a scenic viewpoint of Benham Falls. After enjoying the view, turn around and head back uphill to the trail junction. Retrace the route back to the trailhead.

2.0 Arrive back at the trailhead.

Options: You can hike another 1.5 miles on the Deschutes River Trail to Slough Meadow, or if you are looking for an all-day hike, you can continue another 7.7 miles to the Meadow Day Use Area. Leave a second vehicle at the Meadow Day Use Area for a one-way shuttle option. Travel 6.2 miles west of Bend on the Cascade Lakes Highway (OR 46) and turn left onto gravel FR 100 at the MEADOW PICNIC AREA sign. Continue 1.4 miles to the parking area and trailhead.

9 Big Obsidian Flow Trail

The Big Obsidian Flow Trail is an easy and convenient way to check out Oregon's youngest lava flow. Located in Newberry National Volcanic Monument, this fascinating path crosses the lava flow and highlights the volcanic history of the area. Interpretive signs along the way explain how Native Americans visited the area to collect obsidian for making jewelry and tools.

Distance: 0.7-mile loop
Hiking time: 30 minutes–1 hour
Elevation gain: 300 feet
Trail surface: Paved path, stairs
Best season: Late June through Oct
Other trail users: None
Canine compatibility: Leashed dogs permitted
Fees and permits: A Northwest Forest Pass is required. You can purchase a pass at the entrance booth to the monument or online at https://store.usgs.gov/forest-pass or by calling (800) 270-7504.
Schedule: Open dawn to dusk
Maps: USFS Deschutes National Forest, Newberry Crater Volcanic Monument
USGS map: East Lake, OR

Finding the trailhead: From the intersection of Greenwood Avenue and US 97 (Business) in Bend, travel south on US 97 for 23 miles to a sign for NEWBERRY NATIONAL VOLCANIC MONUMENT AND PAULINA AND EAST LAKES. Turn left on Paulina Lake Road (FR 21) and drive 15.4 miles to the Big Obsidian Trailhead parking area on the right side of the road. GPS: N43 42.694' / W121 16.620'

The Hike

One of the main attractions at the 55,000-acre Newberry National Volcanic Monument is the Big Obsidian Flow

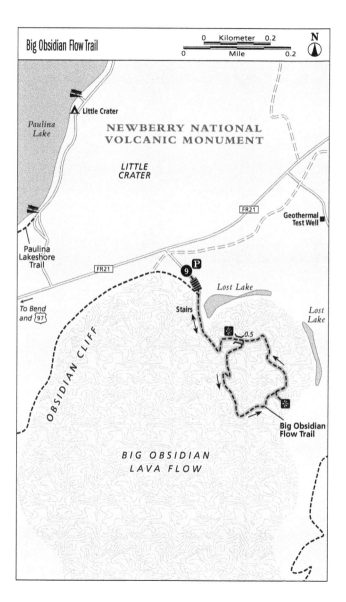

Trail, which provides a fascinating tour of Oregon's youngest lava flow. The trail, which begins as a flat, paved path, offers panoramic views of the flow and includes interpretive signs intended to make understanding the landscape easy. The lava rock is very sharp, so be sure to wear sturdy shoes.

After a short distance the path ascends a steep set of metal stairs and, at the top, arrives at the flow itself—a vast spread of gray pumice interspersed with shiny glasslike boulders of obsidian.

Just past the stairs, the trail comes to a T intersection. From here you can go right or left to begin a 0.3-mile loop. The loop offers outstanding views of 7,984-foot Paulina Peak and Paulina and East Lakes, located at the center of 500-square-mile Newberry Crater.

The 1,300-year-old flow, which covers 1.1 square miles and has an average thickness of 150 feet, began as extremely hot magma (up to 1,600 degrees Fahrenheit) trapped by the Earth's crust 2 to 4 miles underground. The magma eventually found weak points in the Earth's surface, and a violent eruption ensued. Later, as the eruption slowed, the sticky magma began oozing out of the Earth and crawling over the landscape.

One of the more interesting features of the present-day rough and jumbled flow is the glasslike obsidian found on its surface. Due to the way obsidian is formed (through rapid cooling of lava), it is very hard and extremely sharp. These properties were highly valued by Native Americans, who called the rock Isukws (pronounced "eshookwsh"). They made arrowheads, knives, jewelry, ornaments, sculptures, ceremonial objects, and tools out of the obsidian to trade with other tribes for fish, shells, and roots. Artifacts dating back 10,000 years have been found in the monument and surrounding areas. You can read about these relics of the past as you walk the trail.

Miles and Directions

0.0 Start hiking on the paved path by the parking area.

0.1 Ascend a set of metal stairs to the lava flow.

0.2 Turn right to begin the loop portion of the trail.

0.5 Turn right (this is the end of the loop).

0.7 Arrive back at the trailhead.

10 Paulina Lake Loop

This scenic hike follows the Paulina lakeshore in the Newberry National Volcanic Monument.

Distance: 7.5-mile loop
Hiking time: 3-4 hours
Elevation gain: 230 feet
Trail surface: Gravel path, dirt path, and paved road
Best season: Late June through Oct
Other trail users: None
Canine compatibility: Leashed dogs permitted
Fees and permits: A Northwest Forest Pass is required. You can purchase a pass at the entrance booth to the monument or online at https://store.usgs.gov/forest-pass or by calling (800) 270-7504.
Schedule: Open dawn to dusk
Maps: USFS Deschutes National Forest, Newberry Crater Volcanic Monument
USGS map: Paulina Lake, OR

Finding the trailhead: From the intersection of Northwest Franklin and US 97 (Business) in Bend, travel 23 miles south on US 97. Turn left (east) onto FR 21 (Paulina Lake Road). After 11.6 miles you'll pass the entrance booth to the national monument on your left. Continue 1.6 miles past the entrance booth to the Paulina Lakeshore Trailhead on the left. GPS: N43 42.736' / W121 16.565'

The Hike

At first glance, Central Oregon may be characterized by its wide-open spaces, sagebrush- and juniper-scattered plateaus, rounded buttes, forested ridges, and snowcapped mountains. But not far off the main highways are some of the most unique and dramatic features in the world—the remains of volcanic activity that, geologically speaking, occurred fairly recently.

One of the most stunning of these geological features can be seen at 50,000-acre Newberry National Volcanic Monument, located southeast of Bend off US 97. This national preserve was established in 1990 as the volcanic centerpiece of the Central Oregon region. At the heart of this preserve is the 500-square-mile Newberry Caldera crater, which cradles two pristine alpine lakes—Paulina and East.

Paulina Lake (250 feet deep) and East Lake (180 feet deep) were a single, very large lake until lava flows split them apart approximately 6,200 years ago. Today these two lakes are designated as a wildlife refuge, supporting bald eagles, ducks, geese, ospreys, and tundra swans. Mammals roaming the shores and surrounding peaks and valleys include badgers, black bears, deer, elk, and pine martens. Both lakes are popular fishing spots for trout and other fish.

Newberry Volcano is located along a group of faults called the Northwest Rift Zone and is one of the largest shield volcanoes in the United States. Shield volcanoes are formed mainly by fluid lava flows pouring from a central vent to form a broad, gently sloping, dome-shaped cone. The volcano's most recent activity occurred 1,300 years ago, when it deposited more than 170 million cubic yards of obsidian and pumice into what is now called Big Obsidian Flow, located just east of Paulina Lake Lodge.

This fun hike circles Paulina Lake. The route takes you past prime swimming beaches, piles of shiny black obsidian, and stellar views of 7,984-foot Paulina Peak. Be prepared for cool weather—and bring plenty of mosquito repellent.

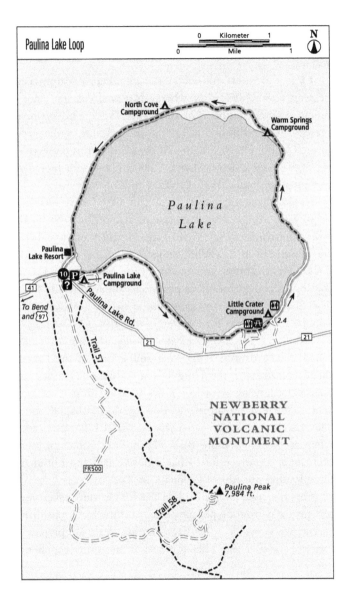

Paulina Lake Loop

North Cove Campground

Warm Springs Campground

Paulina Lake

Paulina Lake Resort

Paulina Lake Campground

Paulina Lake Rd.

Little Crater Campground

2.4

To Bend and 97

Trail 57

NEWBERRY NATIONAL VOLCANIC MONUMENT

FR500

Trail 58

Paulina Peak 7,984 ft.

Miles and Directions

0.0 From the paved parking area, start around the lake in a counterclockwise direction on the signed PAULINA LAKESHORE TRAIL. The trail starts out as a gravel path lined with stones.

0.1 Hike across a paved boat ramp and then continue walking on the signed trail. Not far past this junction, a sign indicates LITTLE CRATER CAMPGROUND 2.5 MILES.

1.5 The trail seems to fade out. Continue following the lakeshore.

1.7 The trail is evident again and becomes a long grassy track next to an inviting sandy beach.

2.2 Arrive at a paved boat ramp that has a restroom and picnic tables. After crossing the paved boat ramp, you'll arrive at a sign that states PAULINA LAKESHORE LOOP TRAIL/TRAIL FOLLOWS ROAD. From this point follow the paved road as it parallels the lakeshore.

2.4 Arrive at the entrance to Little Crater Campground. Continue on the paved road through the campground as it follows the lakeshore.

2.5 Pass a restroom and a water faucet. Follow the road through the campground until it ends. Turn right into a gravel trailhead parking lot and pick up the Paulina Lakeshore Trail. There are two trails at this parking area. Take the trail going left. (FYI: The trail goes around a rocky point with cool lava outcroppings and fantastic views of Paulina Peak. Watch your footing over the next mile—it is rocky and filled with tree roots.)

4.0 Turn right at the trail sign.

4.5 The trail begins climbing a high ridge above the lake for the next 0.5 mile.

5.0 Begin descending the ridge on a series of long sweeping switchbacks back to the lakeshore.

6.9 Pass several vacation cabins on your right. The trail becomes faint here; keep following the lakeshore.

7.0 Turn right onto a gravel road next to the Paulina Lake Resort general store.

7.1 The road becomes pavement.

7.2 Turn left onto the unsigned dirt singletrack trail.

7.3 Turn left onto a paved road and then cross a concrete bridge over Paulina Creek. Immediately after crossing the bridge, turn left and go down a set of stone steps to pick up the unsigned dirt trail.

7.5 Arrive back at the trailhead.

11 Lava Lands Visitor Center Trails

This route combines two trails: the Trail of the Molten Land and the Trail of the Whispering Pines, which are both accessed from the Lava Lands Visitor Center. The first trail takes you on a journey through an amazing lava flow to a viewpoint with spectacular views of the Central Cascade Mountains. The second trail winds through a second-growth ponderosa forest and has interpretive signs explaining the plants, animals, and history of the area.

Distance: 1.4-mile figure eight
Hiking time: 30 minutes–1 hour
Elevation gain: 295 feet
Trail surface: Paved path
Best season: May through Oct
Other trail users: None
Canine compatibility: Leashed dogs permitted

Fees and permits: A Northwest Forest Pass is required. You can purchase a pass online at https://store.usgs.gov/forest-pass or by calling (800) 270-7504.
Schedule: 9 a.m. to 5 p.m.
Maps: Lava Lands Map
USGS map: Lava Butte, OR

Finding the trailhead: From the intersection of Northwest Franklin and US 97 (Business) in Bend, travel 11.2 miles south on US 97 to a LAVA LANDS VISITOR CENTER sign. Turn right (west) and park in the main parking area. GPS: N43 54.591' / W121 21.412'

The Hike

This short hike takes you on a tour of the moonlike landscape of a spectacular lava flow—the result of the eruption of Lava Butte that occurred between 6,000 and 7,000 years ago. When Lava Butte erupted, the lava flowed in three main channels, covering 10 square miles and blocking the Deschutes River in five different locations.

The hike begins adjacent to the Lava Lands Visitor Center, which is filled with exhibits on the area's geology, animals, and plants. A small selection of maps and books is also available. You'll follow the Trail of the Molten Land as it winds through the lava flow. Interpretive signs help identify important features about the lava flow, including surface tubes and lava channels. The basalt that surrounds you on this trail is not as shiny and brilliant as obsidian because it does not contain as much silica (glass), leaving it with a duller appearance. Lava Butte rises sharply from the lava field and is a major landmark on this hike. Lava Butte was created from gas-charged basalt rocks called cinders that were part of a large lava eruption. As these cinders cooled, they formed the butte.

After 0.7 mile you'll arrive at the Phil Brogan Viewpoint. From this high viewpoint you'll have far-reaching views of the immense lava flow and the Central Cascade Mountains. From here you'll complete the short Trail of the Molten Land loop and then continue walking on the Trail of the Whispering Pines. This short interpretive trail weaves through a second-growth forest of ponderosa and lodgepole pines. Interpretive signs describe some of the native plants that grow here, including snowbrush, manzanita, and squaw currant. Native Americans used these plants in a variety of ways. The bark and roots of the snowbrush plant were used as an astringent, manzanita seeds were ground into flour, and parts of the squaw currant were used to cure stomach ailments.

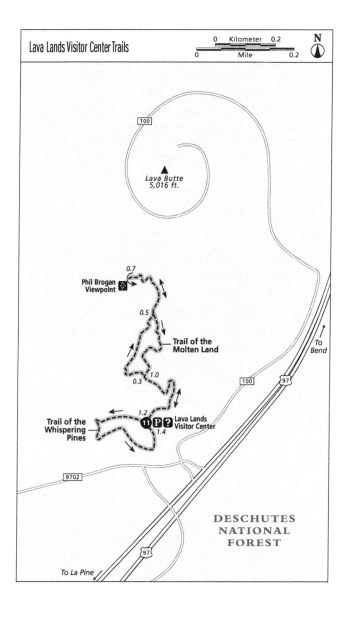

Lava Lands Visitor Center Trails

0   Kilometer   0.2

0   Mile   0.2

N

100

▲
Lava Butte
5,016 ft.

0.7

Phil Brogan
Viewpoint

0.5

Trail of the
Molten Land

1.0

0.3

Trail of the
Whispering
Pines

1.2

🍴 P ❓ Lava Lands
Visitor Center

1.4

9702

100

97

To Bend

DESCHUTES
NATIONAL
FOREST

97

To La Pine

Miles and Directions

0.0 From the main parking area, start walking on a paved path toward the visitor's center. (You'll reach a trail junction before you reach the visitor center.)

Turn left onto the paved path. Continue about another 50 feet to another trail junction and turn right. (The Trail of the Whispering Pines goes left at this junction.) At the next trail junction, continue straight on the signed TRAIL OF THE MOLTEN LAND.

0.3 Turn left at the trail junction.

0.5 Turn left toward the signed PHIL BROGAN VIEWPOINT.

0.7 Arrive at the Phil Brogan Viewpoint. Take a break on the wood benches and soak in the view of the Central Cascade Mountains and the magnificent lava flow. Walk down the viewpoint trail to the junction with the Trail of the Molten Land Trail and turn left.

1.0 The loop portion of the trail ends. Continue straight (left).

1.2 Turn right at the trail junction toward the signed TRAIL OF THE WHISPERING PINES.

1.3 Turn right and continue on the paved Trail of the Whispering Pines.

1.4 Arrive back at the trailhead.

12 Fall River

This beautiful trail follows the course of the crystal-clear, spring-fed Fall River. This uncrowded route takes you through immense groves of ponderosa pine trees and offers many scenic viewpoints of the river where you may see Canada geese, ospreys, and mallard ducks.

Distance: 6.4 miles out and back
Hiking time: 2.5–3.5 hours
Elevation gain: 100 feet
Trail surface: Dirt path, double-track road
Best season: Apr through Nov
Other trail users: Mountain bikers

Canine compatibility: Dogs permitted
Fees and permits: No fees or permits required
Schedule: Open all hours
Maps: USFS Deschutes National Forest
USGS map: Pistol Butte, OR

Finding the trailhead: From the intersection of Greenwood Avenue and US 97 (Business) in Bend, travel 16.7 miles south on US 97. Turn right (west) onto Vandevert Road at the VANDEVERT ROAD/ FALL RIVER sign. Continue for 1 mile to the junction with South Century Drive. Turn left and go 1 mile to the junction with Cascade Lakes Highway (FR 42). Go right and continue 10.4 miles (you'll pass Fall River Campground on the left after 9.7 miles) to an unsigned gravel circular parking area on the left side of the road. A green Forest Service building is also located adjacent to the parking area. GPS: N43 46.1.20' / W121 38.006'

The Hike

Located in the Deschutes National Forest southwest of Bend, Fall River is a beautiful spring-fed river that is stocked with brown, brook, and rainbow trout. The source of the river is situated about 2 miles northwest of Pringle Falls on the Deschutes River. From this location the river meanders northeast for 8 miles until it joins the Deschutes River about 6 miles below Pringle Falls.

This route parallels the course of the river for 3.2 miles. The tour takes you through a forest corridor of stately ponderosa pine trees. These yellow-barked giants are prized for their clear, even grain, which is used for door and window frames. This hardy tree is fire-resistant and survives drought better than any other Northwest tree. The root system is deep and extensively branched, and the tree can survive on only 8 to 12 inches of rain per year. These amazing trees can live to be 400 to 500 years of age and grow to be more than 120 feet tall and 5 feet in diameter.

After 0.7 mile you'll arrive at quiet Fall River Campground. This Forest Service campground has ten tent sites with picnic tables, fire grills, and vault toilets. You'll hike through the campground for 0.1 mile and then continue on the singletrack trail next to Campsite 8. From here the forest deepens, with thick stands of lodgepole pines. These trees are also drought- and fire-resistant and can live in poor soils. They grow very slowly, and it may take a century for a tree to reach a height of 60 feet. Native Americans used the long, thin trunks of these trees as supporting poles for their tepee lodges.

As the trail approaches the river's edge, watch for Canada geese and ducks feeding in the river. Also be on the lookout for ospreys perched on dead tree snags along the river's edge. After 1.2 miles you'll walk on a doubletrack road for 0.4 mile and then turn back onto a singletrack trail until the trail's end and your turnaround point at 3.2 miles.

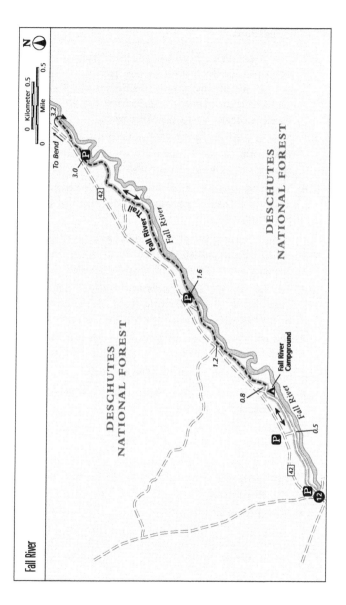

Fall River

Miles and Directions

0.0 Look to your left and begin hiking on the doubletrack road that begins adjacent to a wooden pole fence. Go 75 yards and then veer left onto a smaller doubletrack road. This road soon becomes a wide singletrack trail that takes you through a corridor of large ponderosa pines.

0.5 Arrive at a sign (facing the other way) that states end of trail/parking on road 42. Ignore the sign and continue heading east as the trail parallels Fall River.

0.6 Veer to the right at the brown hiker sign. (FYI: Just past this junction you'll pass a picturesque wooden bridge that spans Fall Creek.)

0.7 Arrive at Fall River Campground Day Use Area. (Restrooms are available on your left.) Turn onto the gravel campground loop road and continue through the campground.

0.8 Veer right on the unsigned singletrack Fall River Trail that begins just to the left of Campsite 8 and takes you through a thick lodgepole pine forest right near the river's edge.

1.2 The trail intersects a red-cinder road. Turn right onto the cinder road.

1.5 Turn right onto an unsigned doubletrack road.

1.6 Turn right onto an unsigned singletrack trail just before the doubletrack road meets a red-cinder road.

3.0 Continue straight across a parking area and continue hiking on the signed FALL RIVER TRAIL.

3.2 Arrive at a rock dam across the river and an end of trail sign. This is your turnaround point. Retrace the route back to your starting point.

6.4 Arrive back at the trailhead.

13 Ray Atkeson Memorial Trail

This hike has gorgeous views of Sparks Lake, South Sister, and Broken Top. The trail parallels the edge of the lake and then winds through a thick lodgepole pine forest and past interesting lava flows. You will also have nice views of Mount Bachelor midway through the hike. This hike is a must-do if you crave beautiful lake and mountain views.

Distance: 2.4-mile loop
Hiking time: 1 hour
Elevation gain: 60 feet
Trail surface: Paved path, dirt path
Best season: Late June through Oct
Other trail users: None
Canine compatibility: Leashed dogs permitted

Fees and permits: A Northwest Forest Pass is required. You can purchase a pass online at https://store.usgs.gov/forest -pass or by calling (800) 270-7504
Schedule: Open all hours
Maps: USFS Deschutes National Forest
USGS map: Broken Top, OR

Finding the trailhead: From Bend travel 26 miles west on the Cascade Lakes Highway (OR 46) to the turnoff for FR 400 at the SPARKS LAKE RECREATION AREA sign. Turn left (south) on FR 400 and go 0.1 mile to a road junction. Bear left on FR 100 toward the SPARKS LAKE BOAT RAMP AND TRAILHEADS sign. Go 1.7 miles and turn left into the Ray Atkeson Memorial Trailhead parking area. GPS: N44 00.791' / W121 44.213'

The Hike

This loop hike takes you past scenic Sparks Lake and through a pine forest with interesting lava outcroppings. The trail is paved and wheelchair accessible for the first 0.4 mile. This hike offers jaw-dropping views of Sparks Lake with South Sister and Broken Top in the background and is named for well-known nature photographer Ray Atkeson. Ray Atkeson was known for his large-format, scenic color photography, and this trail is dedicated to him.

The trail starts by paralleling the shoreline of Sparks Lake, which covers 400 acres and has a depth of 10 feet. Sparks Lake was named for early settler Lige Sparks. The lake is popular with canoeists and kayakers who come here to paddle in the quiet waters, explore the hidden coves, and admire the stunning backdrop of South Sister and Broken Top. After 0.8 mile you have the option to turn left and hike a shorter loop on the signed DAVIS CANYON LOOP TRAIL. Halfway through the hike the path leads you up a short hill where you will have more scenic views of Mount Bachelor, South Sister, and Broken Top. The trail continues winding through a lodgepole pine forest until the loop ends at 2.4 miles.

Miles and Directions

0.0 Start hiking on the signed paved trail. Go 100 yards and turn right onto the signed barrier-free trail.

0.2 Enjoy a spectacular view of Sparks Lake, South Sister, and Broken Top.

0.3 Pass a rest bench with more beautiful mountain and lake views.

0.4 The paved path ends.

0.8 Continue straight on the signed hiking loop. (**Option:** The Davis Canyon Loop Trail goes left at this junction.)

1.4 Arrive at the top of a small knoll that provides a good viewpoint of South Sister, Broken Top, and Mount Bachelor.

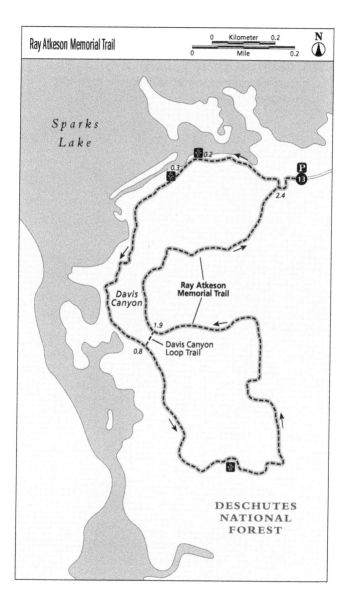

Ray Atkeson Memorial Trail

Sparks Lake

0.2
0.3

P 13

2.4

Davis Canyon

Ray Atkeson Memorial Trail

1.9

0.8
Davis Canyon Loop Trail

DESCHUTES NATIONAL FOREST

N

0   Kilometer   0.2
0   Mile   0.2

1.9 Continue straight (right) at the trail junction (left leads to the trail junction you passed at the 0.8-mile mark).

2.4 The trail turns from dirt to pavement. At the trail junction continue to the right and arrive back at the trailhead in another 100 yards.

14 Green Lakes

This popular hike parallels enchanting Fall Creek and leads you to the Green Lakes Basin. You can admire this group of high Cascade lakes and enjoy views of South Sister and Broken Top.

Distance: 9 miles out and back, with an 11-mile loop option
Hiking time: 4–5 hours
Elevation gain: 1,100 feet
Trail surface: Paved path, dirt path
Best season: Late June through Oct
Other trail users: None
Canine compatibility: Leashed dogs permitted

Fees and permits: A Central Cascades Wilderness Permit is required from June 15 to October 15. You can purchase a pass at www.recreation.gov or by calling (877) 444-6777.
Schedule: Open all hours
Maps: USFS Deschutes National Forest
USGS map: Broken Top, OR

Finding the trailhead: From the intersection of US 97 (Business) and Franklin Avenue in downtown Bend, turn west on Franklin Avenue. Proceed 1.2 miles (Franklin Avenue becomes Riverside Boulevard) to the intersection with Tumalo Avenue. Turn right onto Tumalo Avenue (which becomes Galveston Avenue). Go 0.5 mile and turn left onto Fourteenth Street. This street soon becomes Century Drive, also known as the Cascade Lakes Highway (OR 46). Continue about 27 miles on the highway to the Green Lakes Trailhead parking area on the right side of the road. GPS: N44 1.82' / W121 44.152'

The Hike

This popular route takes you on a tour of the Three Sisters Wilderness along the banks of charming Fall Creek. This boulder-strewn creek is filled with beautiful waterfalls around almost every bend. You'll follow the wide dirt path along the banks of the creek through fragrant forest. The trail also affords views of the Newberry Lava Flow, which erupted from the southeast side of South Sister—youngest of the Three Sisters volcanoes. Shiny black obsidian is present in this amazing lava flow. Because of how obsidian is formed (through rapid cooling of lava), it is very hard and extremely sharp. These properties were highly valued by Native Americans, who called the rock Isukws (pronounced "eshookwsh") and used it to make arrowheads, knives, jewelry, ornaments, sculptures, ceremonial objects, and tools.

After 4.3 miles you'll enter the magnificent Green Lakes Basin. Three greenish-colored lakes fill the basin. Enjoy views of the lakes, South Sister, and Broken Top, and return on the same route. If you are feeling ambitious and want to return on the trail via a loop route, follow the Soda Creek Trail 6.3 miles back to the trailhead. See the "Miles and Directions" section for details. Be sure to arm yourself with mosquito repellent on this hike.

Miles and Directions

- **0.0** Start hiking on smooth, wide Trail 17, which parallels Fall Creek. A sign at the start of the trail indicates MORAINE LAKE 2 MILES/GREEN LAKES 4.5 MILES/PARK MEADOW 9 MILES/SCOTT PASS 21 MILES. The route parallels Fall Creek, which has beautiful waterfalls around almost every bend.

- **2.0** Arrive at a trail junction. Continue straight (right) on the smooth track as it parallels Fall Creek. (The trail that goes left at this junction heads toward Moraine Lake.)

- **4.3** You'll arrive at the Park Meadow/Soda Creek Trail junction. Continue straight to enter the Green Lakes Basin.

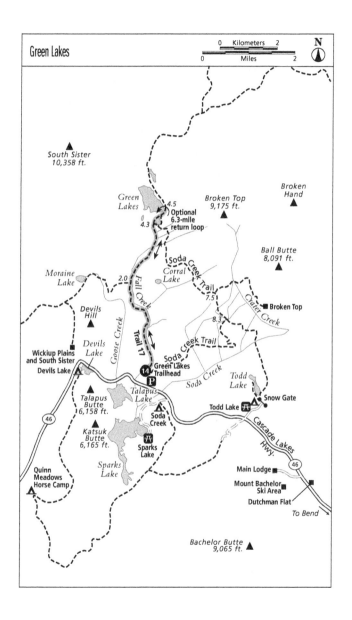

Green Lakes

Kilometers

Miles

N

South Sister
10,358 ft.

Broken Hand

Green Lakes

4.5

Optional
6.3-mile
return loop

4.3

Broken Top
9,175 ft.

Ball Butte
8,091 ft.

Moraine
Lake

2.0

Soda Creek Trail

Corral
Lake

7.5

Broken Top

Crater Creek

Devils
Hill

Fall Creek

Goose Creek

Trail 17

8.3

Soda Creek Trail

Wickiup Plains
and South Sister
Devils Lake

Devils
Lake

14 Green Lakes
Trailhead

Soda Creek

Todd
Lake

Talapus
Lake

Todd Lake

Snow Gate

Talapus
Butte
16,158 ft.

Cascade Lakes Hwy.

46

Katsuk
Butte
6,165 ft.

Soda
Creek

Sparks
Lake

Main Lodge

46

Quinn
Meadows
Horse Camp

Mount Bachelor
Ski Area

Dutchman Flat

To Bend

Bachelor Butte
9,065 ft.

4.5 Enjoy views of the lakes and then turn around and return on the same route.

9.0 Arrive back at the trailhead.

Loop Option: To complete a loop back to the trailhead, you can return on a 6.3-mile route via the Soda Creek Trail. Turn right at the junction at Mile 4.3 toward Park Meadow/Soda Creek. Walk 10 yards and then take another quick right turn toward Soda Creek/Broken Top. Continue climbing up the trail and enjoy awesome views of the Green Lakes to the north. The route skirts the south edge of the 9,175-foot Broken Top peak.

7.5 Turn right toward Soda Creek/Todd Lake. (The Broken Top Trail continues left at this junction.)

8.3 Turn right where a sign indicates SODA CREEK. (The trail that goes left heads toward Todd Lake.) From here you'll continue downhill—be ready to negotiate water crossings at Crater and Soda Creeks.

11.0 Arrive back at the trailhead.

Sisters

15 Eagle Rock Loop

This hike is located just outside of Sisters and is part of a vast network of hiking and mountain bike trails that are part of the Sisters community trail system, Sisters Trail Alliance. This hike takes you through a fragrant ponderosa and lodgepole pine forest and then climbs to the pass of Eagle Rock where you'll have beautiful views of the Central Cascade peaks.

Distance: 5-mile loop
Hiking time: 2–3 hours
Elevation gain: 200 feet
Trail surface: Dirt path
Best season: Mar through Nov
Other trail users: Mountain bikers

Canine compatibility: Leashed dogs permitted
Fees and permits: None
Schedule: Open all hours
Maps: Sisters Trail Map (available at the trailhead or in local stores)
USGS map: Sisters, OR

Finding the trailhead: From US 20 in Sisters, turn south onto Elm Street and travel 0.5 mile and turn left on to Tyee Street. The trailhead is located on the right. There is additional parking on the opposite side of the street. GPS: N44 17.05' / W121 32.98'

The Hike

This hike starts at a small parking area just outside of the Sisters City Limits. There is a signed trail map at the start of the hike. This hike has many signed intersections that are easy to navigate. The hike starts by winding through a ponderosa and lodgepole pine forest. Be on the lookout for mountain bikers who you will share the trail with. After 2.3 miles you'll turned onto the Eagle Rock Pass Trail and start ascending a striking basalt outcropping. As you climb, the trail winds

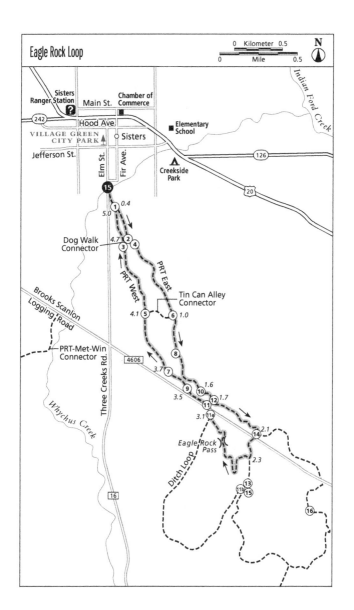

Eagle Rock Loop

through manzanita and rabbitbrush with Indian paintbrush and lupine adding splashes of color to the trail. After 2.7 miles the trail reaches a nice viewpoint of the Three Sisters and other Central Cascade peaks. To see an even more spectacular view you have the option to hike on a spur trail to another great viewpoint, which serves as a great lunch spot. After enjoying the views, the trail descends the other side of this rocky outcropping as you complete a loop back to your starting point.

Miles and Directions

0.0 Start hiking on the main trail that starts at the trailhead.

0.4 Go left and follow the Sisters Trail Marker.

0.6 Go left and follow the Sisters Trail Marker.

0.8 Go right and continue straight across a doubletrack gravel road.

1.0 Continue straight at Trail Junction 6 (the Tin Can Alley Connector goes right).

1.3 Turn left at Trail Junction 8 (the Powerline Connector Trail goes right).

1.6 Go left at Junction 10.

1.7 Go left at Junction 12 and cross a bridge over the irrigation canal.

2.1 Go right on the Boneyard Connector Trail at Junction 14.

2.2 Cross a doubletrack gravel road and continue straight.

2.3 Turn right on the Eagle Rock Pass Trail.

2.5 The trail starts climbing toward the summit of Eagle Rock.

2.7 Arrive at a trail junction. You have the option here of turning right and hiking 0.1 mile to the summit of Eagle Rock, or you can enjoy the view from the main trail.

2.8 Arrive at the summit of Eagle Rock. After admiring the views, turn around and return to the main trail.

2.9 Continue to the right on the main trail and begin descending.

3.1 Turn right at Junction 11A and continue on PRT West Trail toward Sisters.

3.3 Cross a doubletrack gravel road and continue on the signed PRT WEST TRAIL. At the next junction stay to the left and continue on the PRT West Trail.

3.5 Go left at Junction 9 toward Sisters.

3.7 Go left at Junction 7.

4.1 Go left at Junction 5.

4.7 Go left at Junction 3.

5.0 Arrive back at the trailhead.

16 Whychus Creek

This hike takes you along the banks of scenic Whychus Creek past small waterfalls and big rock pools in a gorgeous ponderosa pine forest.

Distance: 6.8 miles out and back
Hiking time: 3-4 hours
Elevation gain: 550 feet
Trail surface: Dirt path
Best season: Year-round; snow may be present during the winter months.

Other trail users: Mountain bikers
Canine compatibility: Dogs permitted
Fees and permits: None
Schedule: Open all hours
Maps: Green Trails No 590, Sisters
USGS map: North Sister, OR

Finding the trailhead: From US 20 in Sisters, turn south onto Elm Street and travel 4.1 miles on Elm Street, which turns into Three Creek Road (FR 16), to a turnoff on the right side of the road marked by a brown hiker sign. GPS: N44 14.116' / W121 33.71'

The Hike

This trail travels parallel to the scenic 41-mile-long Whychus Creek. The name Whychus is derived from the Sahaptin language and means "the place we cross the water."

The source of this creek is at the base of the Three Sisters Mountains, and it flows through the Deschutes Basin until it joins the Deschutes River near Lake Billy Chinook. Historically the creek provided important habitat for salmon, trout, and steelhead. Low water levels, obstacles blocking fish, and habitat degradation caused the fish to disappear from certain sections of the creek. Over the past several years, habitat

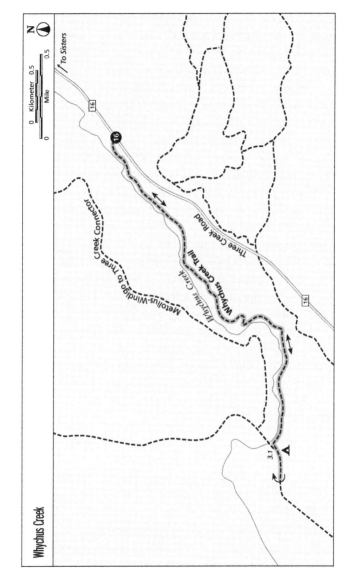

Whychus Creek

N

0 Kilometer 0.5

0 Mile 0.5

To Sisters

16

16

16

Three Creek Road

Whychus Creek Trail

Whychus Creek

Metolius-Windigo to Three Creek Connector

3.1

restoration has become a priority for this important watershed, and the Deschutes River Conservancy has worked with the Deschutes Land Trust and Upper Deschutes Watershed Council to reintroduce fish into the creek.

The route follows the picturesque creek through large stands of stately ponderosa pine trees. The creek has a character of its own due to its many scenic geologic features created by glacial and volcanic events. As you hike the trail you will see numerous small waterfalls, a variety of channel shapes, giant boulders, rock spires, and channel beds of polished rock with potholes. At 0.2 mile you will pass by an old irrigation canal and canal switch that diverted water from the creek for irrigation. After 1.8 miles the trail descends a rocky embankment and then continues to parallel the creek. At 2.2 miles you'll pass a nice viewpoint of a small waterfall. After 3.1 miles you'll arrive at the junction with the Metolius-Windigo Trail. This trail is popular with horseback riders. After the trail junction you'll pass a campground on the left that is sheltered by the canopy of beautiful old ponderosa pine trees. Continue left on the Whychus Creek Trail until it ends at 3.4 miles. This is your turnaround point. Retrace your route back to the trailhead.

Miles and Directions

- **0.0** Start hiking on the signed trail that indicates METOLIUS-WINDIGO TRAIL 2¾, 800 ROAD TRAILHEAD 3 MILES.
- **0.2** Pass an old irrigation canal and canal switch that was once used for irrigation.
- **1.8** Traverse down a rocky hillside.
- **2.2** Arrive at a nice viewpoint of a small waterfall.
- **3.1** Arrive at a trail junction. Turn left (the Metolius-Windigo Trail goes right). You will pass a campground on your left.

3.4 Arrive at the route's turnaround point. Retrace the route back to the trailhead.

6.8 Arrive back at the trailhead.

17 Chush Falls

The route travels high above the swirling Whychus Creek through a stark lodgepole pine forest that was blackened by the Pole Creek Fire. It climbs to a viewpoint of Chush Falls with opportunities to continue another 0.5 mile on an unofficial trail to a viewpoint of Middle Falls and Upper Cascades Falls.

Distance: 5.0 miles out and back
Hiking time: 2.5–3.5 hours
Elevation gain: 550 feet
Trail surface: Dirt path
Best season: June through Oct
Other trail users: None
Canine compatibility: Dogs permitted
Fees and permits: A Northwest Forest Pass is required. You can purchase a pass at https://store.usgs.gov/forest-pass or by calling (800) 270-7504. A free wilderness permit is also required and can be obtained at the trailhead.
Schedule: Open all hours
Maps: Green Trails No. 590, Sisters
USGS map: Trout Creek Butte, OR

Finding the trailhead: From the intersection of US 20 in Sisters, turn south onto Elm Street (FR 16) and travel 7 miles. Turn right onto FR 1514 and travel 3 miles to a road fork. Stay to the right and travel 2 miles to the junction with FR 600. Turn left and continue on FR 600 for 1 mile to the trailhead parking area. GPS: N44 10.64' / W121 40.01'

The Hike

Start hiking on this dirt path as it travels through a thick lodgepole pine forest that was blackened in the Pole Creek Fire. The stark, blackened trees are a sharp contrast to the

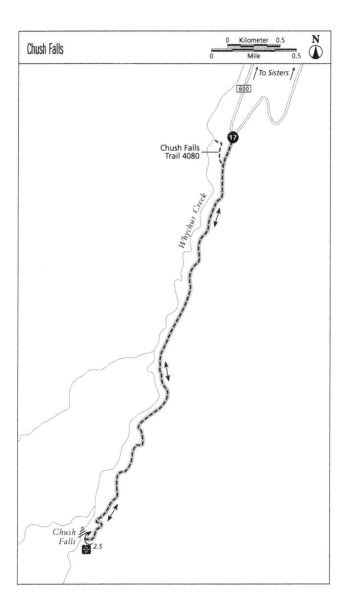

bright purple lupine, Indian paintbrush, and bright green manzanita that line the trail. As you hike, you can catch glimpses of Whychus Creek flowing through the canyon at a fast pace in the canyon below.

Between 1.5 miles and 1.7 miles you'll cross a series of small creeks. If you have your dog with you, these are good opportunities to let him cool off. After 2.1 miles the trail starts climbing a steep hill that winds through a green canopy that was not impacted by the fire. After 2.4 miles you'll arrive at a nice viewpoint of Chush Falls. You can turn around here or another option is to go past the TRAIL END sign and hike another 0.5 mile up the river on an unofficial trail where you'll pass Middle Falls and then arrive at Upper Cascades Falls. Return on the same route.

Miles and Directions

0.0 Start hiking on the signed CHUSH FALLS TRAIL. Be sure to fill out a self-issue wilderness permit.

1.6 Cross a side creek over a log.

1.7 Cross a series of two more side creeks.

2.5 Arrive at a viewpoint of Chush Falls. Retrace the route back to the trailhead. (**Option:** You can hike another 0.5 mile upstream past Middle Falls to a viewpoint of Upper Cascades Falls.)

5.0 Arrive back at the trailhead.

18 Park Meadow

This hike takes you into a high-alpine meadow in the Three Sisters Wilderness with gorgeous views of Broken Top and South Sister.

Distance: 7.2 miles out and back
Hiking time: 2.5–3.5 hours
Elevation gain: 700 feet
Trail surface: Dirt path
Best season: Late June through Oct
Other trail users: Equestrians
Canine compatibility: Leashed dogs permitted

Fees and permits: A free wilderness permit is required from June 15 to October 15. The self-issue permit can be obtained at the permit station, located on the trail 0.8 mile from the trailhead.
Schedule: Open all hours
Maps: USFS Deschutes National Forest
USGS map: Broken, OR

Finding the trailhead: From US 20 in Sisters, turn south onto Elm Street (this street becomes FR 16) and travel 14 miles to the Park Meadow Trailhead on the right side of the road. Turn right at the trailhead sign onto a rough gravel road. (If you are driving a passenger car, you'll need to be careful on this rocky, rutted road.) If you are in a passenger car, you can travel for 1 mile on this dirt road and park beside the road, then walk the remaining 0.1 mile to the trailhead. If you have a high-clearance vehicle, you can drive the 1.1 miles to the trailhead. GPS: N44 14.116' / W121 33.712'

The Hike

This route begins by winding through a thick forest of mountain hemlock, cedar, and blue spruce. Mountain hemlock can be found growing at elevations of 3,500 to 6,000 feet and is often confused with western hemlock. This hardy tree differs from the western hemlock by having thick needles that fan out in bushy clusters. It also has 2-inch-long cones and blue-green foliage. In contrast, the western hemlock has flat needles that are shaped in an open spray, cones that are an inch or less in length, and yellow-green foliage. Mountain hemlocks are also characterized by their deep, furrowed bark and are usually the first trees to grow at timberline. It's not uncommon for a mature branch to touch the ground and take root as a new tree. The parent tree then shelters the new tree from the harsh high-altitude environment.

Be sure to obtain a wilderness permit at the self-issue station at 0.8 mile. After walking for about 2 miles, you'll get sneak peeks of Broken Top and South Sister above the tree line. At 2.5 miles, cross a log bridge over bubbling Whychus Creek—a major source of irrigation for Central Oregon farmers and ranchers. After 3.4 miles arrive at Park Meadow, where you'll have unsurpassed views of Broken Top and South Sister from the gorgeous wildflower-filled meadow. Continue walking through the meadow to your turnaround point at 3.6 miles. (*Note:* Be sure to arm yourself with mosquito repellent on this hike.)

Miles and Directions

0.0 Start hiking at the trailhead sign that indicates PARK MEADOW 3¾ GREEN LAKES TRAIL 6¾.

0.8 Cross a shallow stream and then arrive at a four-way junction. Continue straight toward Park Meadow. Be sure to pick up a free self-issue wilderness permit at the permit station at this junction.

1.2 Cross a log bridge over a bubbling creek. Continue hiking on the forested trail, which has periodic rocky sections.

2.5 Cross a log bridge over Whychus Creek.

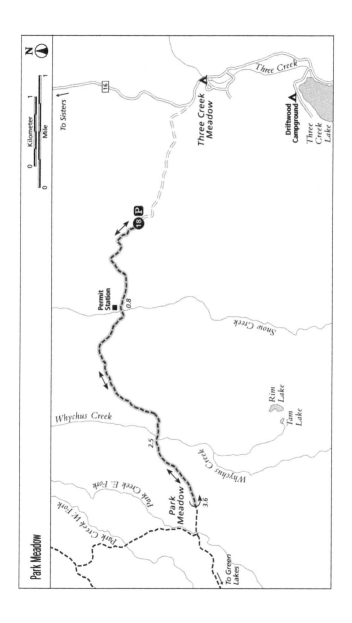

3.4 Arrive at Park Meadow. To continue across the meadow, cross a log bridge over a fast-flowing creek and continue on the trail across the meadow for about another 0.2 mile.

3.6 Arrive at the route's turnaround point. Be sure to bask in the sun and enjoy the spectacular mountain views before retracing your route to your starting point.

7.2 Arrive back at the trailhead.

19 Head of the Metolius River

This popular route takes you to a spectacular viewpoint of the natural spring that is the source for the Metolius River.

Distance: 0.5 mile out and back
Hiking time: 30 minutes
Elevation gain: None
Trail surface: Paved path
Best season: Open year-round. Snow may be present during the winter months.
Other trail users: None

Canine compatibility: Leashed dogs permitted
Fees and permits: No fees or permits required
Schedule: Open all hours
Maps: USFS Deschutes National Forest
USGS map: Black Butte, OR

Finding the trailhead: From Sisters travel 10 miles west on US 20 to the junction with FR 14. Turn right onto FR 14 toward Camp Sherman. Continue 2.8 miles to a Y junction. Turn right toward the signed campgrounds. Continue 1.6 miles and turn left onto FR 1400–140. Continue 0.1 mile to a paved parking area and the trailhead. GPS: N44 26.037' / W121 38.065'

The Hike

This short hike follows a wide paved path to a bubbling spring that is the source of the Metolius River. Picnic tables and restrooms are located at the trailhead. Many visitors hike this short route and then eat lunch underneath the shady canopy of the towering ponderosa pines.

The path is framed with a decorative split-rail fence and travels through a parklike stand of ponderosa pine trees to a viewpoint of the Metolius Spring. From the viewpoint you'll have a stunning view of a grassy meadow, with snowcapped

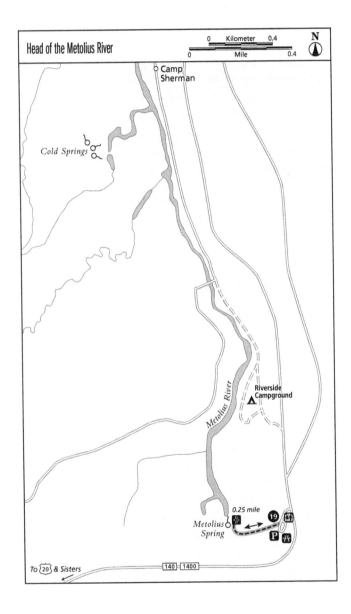

Head of the Metolius River

0 Kilometer 0.4
0 Mile 0.4

N

Camp
Sherman

Cold Springs

Metolius River

Riverside
Campground

0.25 mile

Metolius
Spring

19

P

To 20 & Sisters

140 1400

Mount Jefferson in the background. You'll retrace the route back to the trailhead.

Miles and Directions

0.0 Start hiking on the wheelchair-accessible paved path.

0.25 Arrive at a viewpoint of the headwaters of the Metolius River. Retrace the route back to the trailhead.

0.5 Arrive back at the trailhead.

20 West Metolius River

This trail traces the banks of the clear, fast-moving Metolius River and meanders through a lush riparian ecosystem of bright wildflowers and riverside vegetation.

The spring-fed river rushes over lava to create swirling rapids and big eddies that are home to various species of salmon and trout. At the turnaround point is the Wizard Falls Fish Hatchery, a great place to take a break and explore. Water and restrooms are available at the fish hatchery. Trails continue to follow the river north on both sides for longer hike options.

Distance: 5.0 miles out and back (with longer options)
Hiking time: 2-3 hours
Elevation gain: 200 feet
Trail surface: Dirt path
Best season: Open year-round. The driest months are June through Oct.
Other trail users: None

Canine compatibility: Leashed dogs permitted
Fees and permits: No fees or permits required
Schedule: Open all hours
Maps: USFS Deschutes National Forest
USGS maps: Black Butte, OR; Candle Creek, OR; Prairie Farm Spring, OR

Finding the trailhead: From Sisters head 10 miles west on US 20 to Camp Sherman Road (FR 14). Turn right (north) and travel 2.7 miles to the junction with FR 1419. Turn left and go 2.3 miles to another road junction and stop sign. Continue straight (you're now on FR 1420) for another 3.4 miles to the junction with FR 400. Turn right onto FR 400 toward Lower Canyon Creek Campground; go through the campground to the signed trailhead parking area. GPS: N44 30.078' / W121 38.455'

The Hike

The Metolius River, known for its world-class fly fishing, originates as a natural spring at the base of Black Butte before winding its way north through the Metolius Basin and into Lake Billy Chinook. Numerous springs, fed via porous volcanic rock high in the Central Cascade Mountains, continue to feed the river along its length, keeping the flow rate fairly steady at 1,200 to 1,800 cubic feet per second.

The Northern Paiute and Tenino Indians were the first people known to inhabit the Metolius Basin. They fished for salmon, hunted deer and small game, and gathered nuts and berries on the slopes of Black Butte. In the mid-nineteenth century several well-known explorers traveled through the area.

Among them were Captain John Charles Fremont, who passed through in 1843, and Lieutenant Henry Larcom Abbott, who arrived in 1855 as a surveyor for the Pacific Railroad.

Homesteading in the Metolius Valley didn't occur until 1881. Settlers were attracted to the area by the thick timber and abundant grass that provided good grazing for livestock. The numerous springs and creeks in the valley ensured a plentiful supply of water. In 1893, with the passage of the Forest Reserve Act by President Grover Cleveland, the Metolius Valley became part of the Cascade Range Forest Reserve. In 1908 the area was incorporated into Deschutes National Forest.

If you want to explore this beautiful river, the West Metolius River Trail is the easiest way to do it. The trail starts at Canyon Creek Campground, located approximately 20 miles northwest of Sisters, and continues a scenic journey

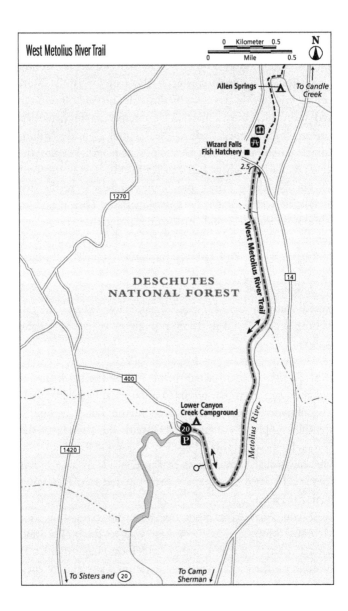

West Metolius River Trail

0 Kilometer 0.5
0 Mile 0.5

N

Allen Springs ▲ To Candle Creek

Wizard Falls Fish Hatchery ■

2.5

1270

West Metolius River Trail

DESCHUTES NATIONAL FOREST

14

400

Lower Canyon Creek Campground ▲

20 P

1420

Metolius River

To Sisters and 20

To Camp Sherman

to Wizard Falls Fish Hatchery. Along the way there is lush streamside greenery, including pinkish-lavender streambank globemallow and bright orange, fragrant honeysuckle, as well as open forest dotted with purple lupine, crimson columbine, lavender-tufted thistle, and white-headed yarrow. Large ponderosa pines shade the path, and the river's deep rock pools and logs provide a haven for trout and salmon. After 2.5 miles the trail arrives at Wizard Falls Fish Hatchery. This is a great place to rest, and tour the hatchery, before the return trip to the trailhead. Restrooms and water are available here.

Miles and Directions

0.0   Start this river hike at the WOOD WEST METOLIUS RIVER TRAIL sign located in the Lower Canyon Creek Campground. A sign indicates that you'll reach Wizard Falls in 2.5 miles.

0.3   Look off to the right to view an amazing natural spring that splashes into the river from underground.

2.5   Arrive at Wizard Falls Fish Hatchery. If you are feeling curious, take the time to explore the fish hatchery before you head back to the trailhead. Water and restrooms are available here. (**Option:** If you want to enjoy a longer river route, you can continue on the trail on the west or east side of the river for about 5 more miles.)

5.0   Retrace your route and arrive back at the trailhead.

21 Lava River Trail–Dee Wright Observatory

This route explores the moonlike landscape of the Yapoah Crater Lava Flow in the Mount Washington Wilderness. As an added bonus, you can explore the unique Dee Wright Observatory.

Distance: 0.5-mile loop
Hiking time: 30 minutes–1 hour
Elevation gain: 200 feet
Trail surface: Paved path
Best season: July through Oct
Other trail users: None
Canine compatibility: Leashed dogs permitted

Fees and permits: No fees or permits required
Schedule: Open all hours
Maps: Mount Washington Wilderness map
USGS map: Mount Washington, OR

Finding the trailhead: From Sisters travel west on US 242 (the McKenzie Highway) for 14.4 miles to a paved parking area on the left side of the road. GPS: N44 15.613' / W121 48.094'

The Hike

This hike explores the western edge of the Yapoah Crater Lava Flow. This incredible lava flow, 8 miles long and a mile wide, is thought to have erupted from Yapoah Crater as recently as 2,700 years ago. The lava that makes up this flow is called AA lava (pronounced *Ah-Ah*) or black lava. This type of lava is made up of basalt and has a rough, jagged surface. This rough surface is caused when the upper layers of lava cool quickly, while the lower layers are still flowing.

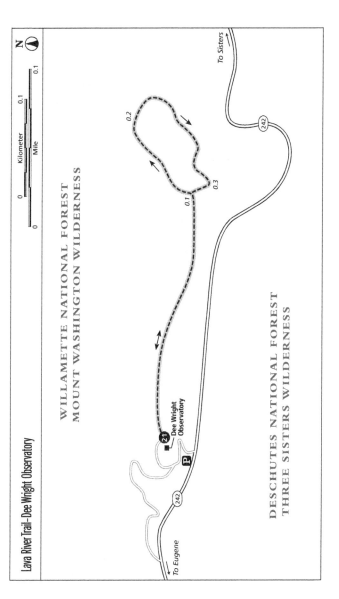

Lava River Trail–Dee Wright Observatory

You'll follow the paved path through the lava flow on a short 0.5-mile loop. When you finish the loop, you can explore the Dee Wright Observatory. The observatory was built by the Civilian Conservation Corps and named for an early-1900s Forest Service packer and mountain guide. The observatory's arched windows frame eleven Cascade peaks.

Miles and Directions

0.0 Start the hike by crossing the highway and turning right on the paved Lava River Trail. (If you go left you can walk up a series of short switchbacks to view the Dee Wright Observatory.)

0.1 Turn left to begin the loop portion of the trail.

0.2 Pass a rest bench on the right.

0.3 Finish the loop. Go left to return to the trailhead.

0.5 Arrive back at the trailhead. Continue straight and walk up the paved spiral path to view the Dee Wright Observatory. After enjoying the views, head back to the parking area.

22 Matthieu Lakes Loop

This is a scenic mountain lake hike where you will walk through a shady hemlock forest to North and South Matthieu Lakes. These high lakes are great for swimming in July and August and have established campsites if you decide you want to turn this popular day hike into an overnight trip. In addition to enjoying the views of these high lakes, you will have a panoramic view of all the Central Cascade peaks on the return portion of this loop hike.

Distance: 6.2-mile loop
Hiking time: 3-4 hours
Elevation gain: 880 feet
Trail surface: Dirt path
Best season: July through Oct
Other trail users: None
Canine compatibility: Dogs are permitted. They must be leashed July 15 through Sept 15.

Fees and permits: Self-issue wilderness permits are required from June 15 to October 15. The permits are available at the trailhead.
Schedule: Open all hours
Maps: Green Trails No. 622, Broken Top Sisters
USGS map: North Sister, OR

Finding the trailhead: From US 20 in Sisters turn onto State Route 242 (McKenzie Pass Highway) for 14.2 miles. Turn left at the LAVA CAMP LAKE AND THE PACIFIC CREST TRAIL sign. Continue 0.3 mile and turn right into the signed PACIFIC CREST TRAIL PARKING LOT. GPS: N44 14.116' / W121 33.71'

The Hike

This is a great hike to bring your dogs on and to enjoy a cool swim on a hot summer day! The hike starts on the Lava Camp Lake Trail and then intersects with the Pacific Crest

Trail after 0.2 mile. If you are hiking in June or July, you may still see snowmelt ponds along this section of the trail. At 0.9 mile you'll cross a small creek and then join up with the North Matthieu Lake Trail. After 1.1 miles the trail skirts a lava field and then starts climbing. After 2.1 miles you'll arrive at a spur trail that takes you to the scenic shores of North Matthieu Lake. Take the time to go for a swim and enjoy the views of this scenic lake. If you feel like exploring, follow the perimeter trail around the lake. After enjoying the lake, you'll continue climbing on a series of switchbacks until you intersect with the Pacific Crest Trail. Continue on the Pacific Crest Trail until you intersect with a spur trail leading to South Matthieu Lake. Once you reach the lakeshore you'll have a nice view of the rocky peak of North Sister. From here you'll continue on the Pacific Crest Trail. The trail opens up out of the forest and you'll have some nice views of the Central Cascade Mountains. You'll continue descending on the Pacific Crest Trail until you reach the junction with Lava Camp Lake Trail 4060, which you'll follow for 0.2 mile back to the trailhead.

Miles and Directions

0.0   Start hiking on the signed LAVA CAMP LAKE TRAIL 4060.

0.2   Turn left (south) on the signed PACIFIC CREST TRAIL 2000.

0.9   Cross a small creek and turn right on North Matthieu Lake Trail 4062 and slowly start climbing.

1.1   Start hiking on the edge of a lava field past several snow-melt ponds. (*Note:* Snow can be present on the trail in early July.)

2.0   Arrive at a spur trail that will take you down to North Matthieu Lake. Turn right on the spur trail.

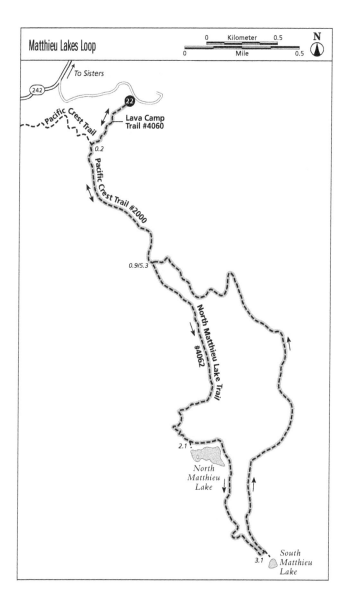

Matthieu Lakes Loop

0 Kilometer 0.5
0 Mile 0.5

N

To Sisters

242

Pacific Crest Trail

22

Lava Camp Trail #4060

0.2

Pacific Crest Trail #2000

0.9/5.3

North Matthieu Lake Trail #4062

2.1

North Matthieu Lake

3.1

South Matthieu Lake

2.1 Arrive at North Matthieu Lake shore. After viewing the lake, return to the main trail.

3.0 Arrive at an intersection with the Pacific Crest Trail.

3.1 At the trail junction turn right to view South Matthieu Lake. You will also have nice views of North Sister. After viewing the lake, return to the main trail.

5.3 At the trail junction, turn right and continue hiking on the Pacific Crest Trail 2000.

6.0 Turn right at the signed LAVA CAMP LAKE TRAIL 4060.

6.2 Arrive back at the trailhead.

23 Little Belknap Crater

This stretch of the Pacific Crest Trail traverses rock-strewn, moonlike terrain on its way to the summit of Little Belknap Crater. Along the way you'll pass lava rock, lava tubes, and fascinating caves. And from the summit you can enjoy views of the Three Sisters, Mount Washington, Black Crater, and many other Cascade peaks.

Distance: 5.0 miles out and back (with longer options)
Hiking time: 3-4 hours
Elevation gain: 975 feet
Trail surface: Dirt path and lava scree
Best season: July through Oct
Other trail users: None
Canine compatibility: Dogs permitted. However, this hike is not recommended for dogs due to the sharp lava scree, which can cut your dog's feet, and no access to shade or water.
Fees and permits: A free self-issue wilderness permit is required and is available at the trailhead.
Schedule: Open all hours
Maps: Green Trails No. 589 Three Fingered Jack, Green Trails No. 590 Sisters
USGS map: Mount Washington, OR

Finding the trailhead: From Sisters travel 14.9 miles west on the McKenzie Highway (OR 242) to the Pacific Crest Trail 2000 Trailhead, located on the right (north) side of the road. (A very small hiker sign marks the trailhead.) (*Note:* Depending on the winter snow conditions, the McKenzie Highway may not open until mid-July.) GPS: N44 15.589' / W121 48.305'

The Hike

The rugged character of Central Oregon's lava country is nowhere better represented than on this hike to the summit of Little Belknap Crater. The rich history of the area begins with the highway to the trailhead. The McKenzie Highway (OR 242) is a gorgeous scenic byway with spectacular views of mountains, lava fields, and endless blue sky—a great introduction to the hike you're about to take.

When gold was discovered in eastern Oregon and Idaho in the 1860s, settlers made a push to find a route that connected the Willamette Valley on the west side of the Cascades to the land on the east. In 1862 Felix Scott and his brother Marion led a party of forty men, sixty oxen, and nine hundred head of cattle and horses across McKenzie Pass, blazing what would later become the Scott Trail. An extremely rough trail, the Scott Trail required almost five days for travel from Eugene in the Willamette Valley to the small town of Sisters in Central Oregon. A toll road was built in 1872 that traveled up Lost Creek Canyon, traversed the rough lava beds, and ended at the Deschutes River.

Today the road is paved and toll-free. It also happens to pass the Dee Wright Observatory (14.5 miles west of Sisters), built by the Civilian Conservation Corps and named for an early 1900s Forest Service packer and mountain guide. The observatory's arched windows frame eleven Cascade peaks. A paved half-mile walkway offers an easy means to explore the eerie moonscape of the Belknap lava flow. The trail is complemented by interpretive signs detailing the area's unique geology. Signs of the old McKenzie Highway, which once crossed the flow, are visible from this vantage point.

When you've had enough of the observatory, continue on to the trailhead for Little Belknap Crater. The trail (95 percent of which is the Pacific Crest Trail) leads through the heart of the Mount Washington Wilderness and its rugged lava formations, craters, and extinct volcanoes. The route begins rather innocently as it winds through an open forest. But within a mile, things change drastically. Soon the forest is replaced by a grayish-black lava flow practically devoid of life, except for the rare hardy tree that has managed to sink its roots through the jumbled basalt rocks.

The flow was created more than 2,900 years ago when hot liquid basalt poured from Belknap Crater, the large cinder cone to the west. Approximately 20 years later a second eruption sprung out of Little Belknap Crater, located directly north of the trailhead. A third phase of eruptions occurred a little more than a thousand years later from the northeast base of Belknap Crater, releasing lava 9 miles west into the McKenzie River Valley.

After 2.2 miles of hiking through this mysterious maze of rock, you come to a trail junction and go right. In 0.2 mile you pass a deep lava tube on your left. If you approach the edge of the tube and look in (be careful—it's quite a drop-off), you can feel the cool air escaping from deep within the earth.

From the lava tube, hike a steep and dramatic 0.1 mile to the top of Little Belknap Crater. The trail surface is loose and crumbly, and piles of gray rock mingle with the bright-red cinders that form much of the crater. When you reach the top, you can enjoy magnificent views of Belknap Crater, Mount Washington, Black Crater, and the Three Sisters Mountains. The summit of Little Belknap Crater is your turnaround point. If you're backpacking, continue on the Pacific Crest Trail as it winds its way north through the magnificent lava country of the Mount Washington Wilderness.

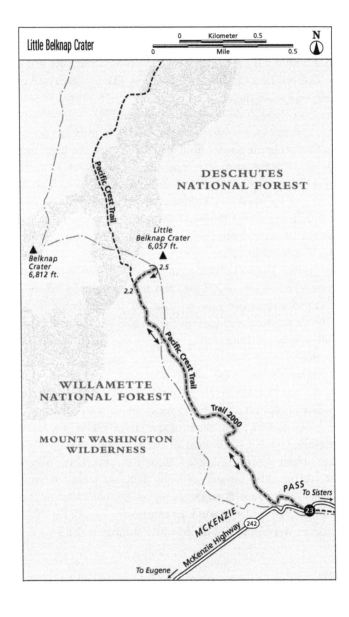

Miles and Directions

0.0 Start hiking on the signed PACIFIC CREST TRAIL 2000. (*Note:* Be sure to fill out the free self-issue wilderness permit at the trailhead.)

0.8 Begin walking on the lava flow.

2.2 Come to a trail junction and turn right to hike to the summit of Little Belknap Crater.

2.4 Pass a lava tube on your left.

2.5 Reach the summit and enjoy sweeping views of Belknap Crater, Mount Washington, Black Crater, and the Three Sisters. Turn around here and retrace your route back to the trailhead. (***Option:*** Continue north on the Pacific Crest Trail and explore more of the Mount Washington Wilderness. Return to your starting point on the same route.)

5.0 Arrive back at the trailhead.

Option: After summiting Little Belknap Crater, return to the junction with the Pacific Crest Trail and turn right. Continue north on the Pacific Crest Trail and explore more of the Mount Washington Wilderness.

24 Hand Lake

This short, scenic route takes you to a small alpine lake, with gorgeous views of snowcapped Mount Washington.

Distance: 1.0 mile out and back
Hiking time: 30 minutes–1 hour
Elevation gain: 100 feet
Trail surface: Dirt path
Best season: July through Oct
Other trail users: None
Canine compatibility: Dogs permitted

Fees and permits: A free self-issue wilderness permit is required and is available at the trailhead.
Schedule: Open all hours
Maps: Green Trails No. 589 Three Fingered Jack and No. 621 Three Sisters
USGS map: North Sister, OR

Finding the trailhead: From Sisters turn west onto the McKenzie Highway (OR 242) and travel 19.3 miles to a gravel pullout on the left side of the road, marked by a brown hiker symbol. GPS: N44 13.499' / W121 52.308'

The Hike

Begin this hike by crossing the highway (use caution) to the signed trailhead. Start hiking on the dirt path as it descends through a thick stand of hemlock and lodgepole pine dotted with purple lupine. After 0.5 mile you'll emerge from the woods into a scenic high-alpine meadow.

Take time to explore the rustic three-sided wood shelter and to walk on a side trail down to the lake's edge. From here you'll have outstanding views of the pointy summit of Mount Washington. Retrace the route back to the trailhead. Be armed with mosquito repellent on this hike.

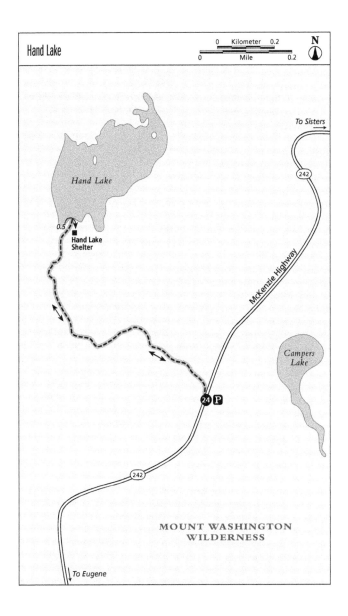

Hand Lake

0 Kilometer 0.2
0 Mile 0.2

N

To Sisters

242

Hand Lake

0.5

Hand Lake
Shelter

McKenzie Highway

Campers
Lake

24 P

242

To Eugene

MOUNT WASHINGTON
WILDERNESS

Miles and Directions

0.0   Cross OR 242 and fill out a free wilderness permit at the signed trailhead. Start walking on the dirt path.

0.5   Arrive at a three-sided wood shelter. Follow a side trail down to the lake's edge. Retrace your route back to the trailhead.

1.0   Arrive back at the trailhead.

25 Canyon Creek Meadows Loop

This very popular loop route takes you on a tour of a high-alpine meadow, with bubbling Canyon Creek flowing through it. In addition, you'll enjoy spectacular views of the jagged spires of Three Fingered Jack.

Distance: 5.2-mile loop
Hiking time: 2.5–3.5 hours
Elevation gain: 675 feet
Trail surface: Dirt path
Best season: July through Oct
Other trail users: None
Canine compatibility: Leashed dogs permitted
Fees and permits: A Northwest Forest Pass is required. You can purchase a pass online at https://store.usgs.gov/forest -pass or by calling (800)

270-7504. A Central Cascades Wilderness Permit is required from June 15 to October 15 for both day and overnight use at this trailhead. Check out https:// recreation.gov or call (877) 444-6777 for more information.
Schedule: Open all hours
Maps: Green Trails No. 589 Three Fingered Jack and No. 557 Mount Jefferson
USGS maps: Three Fingered Jack, OR; Marion Lake, OR

Finding the trailhead: From Sisters travel west on US 20 for 12 miles to Jack Lake Road (FR 12). Turn right and travel 4.3 miles on Jack Lake Road to the junction with FR 1230. Turn left on FR 1230 and go 1.7 miles. At the next road junction, continue left on FR 1234 and continue 5 miles to the trailhead. GPS: N44 23.679' / W121 38.839'

The Hike

High mountain scenery is the highlight of this popular trail. The route takes you past Jack Lake and then enters spectacular Canyon Creek Meadows. Jack Lake covers about 7 acres and is host to a nice campground.

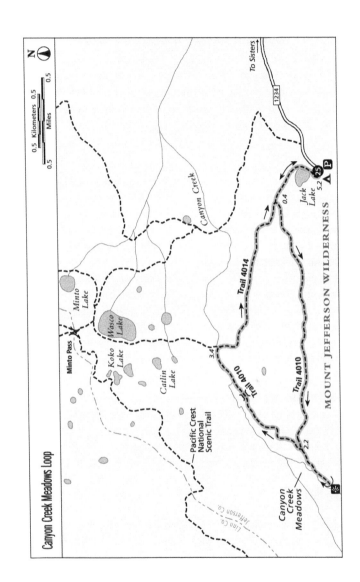

Canyon Creek Meadows Loop

This hike offers you opportunities to view meadows filled with a profusion of bright purple lupine and brilliant red Indian paintbrush blooms in the summer. Along this trail you will also have the opportunity to enjoy a stunning view of the craggy spires of 7,841-foot Three Fingered Jack—named in honor of Joaquin Murietta, an aspiring gold rusher with a mutilated, three-fingered hand. The spires rise abruptly out of Central Oregon's Mount Jefferson Wilderness to form a geologic slide of time. Hundreds of thousands of years ago, the mountain—formed by hot basaltic lava flows—resembled a broad, dome-shaped cone. Since that time, volcanic activity and glaciations have left the southern side of the peak a skeleton of its previous majesty. Today the formation is what geologists call a shield volcano. Bring plenty of mosquito repellent with you on this hike. Also, try to hike this trail during the week to avoid the weekend crowds.

Miles and Directions

0.0 Start hiking on the singletrack trail signed for CANYON CREEK MEADOWS. The trail travels past Jack Lake.

0.4 Turn toward Canyon Creek on Trail 4010. This trail is marked as a one-way loop.

2.2 Arrive at a trail junction at Canyon Creek and a large, picturesque meadow. Turn right and continue on the one-way trail.

2.5 Cross a bridge.

2.9 Cross the creek.

3.4 At the trail junction, turn right onto Trail 4014.

4.8 Turn left onto Trail 4010 toward Jack Lake.

5.2 Arrive back at the trailhead.

26 Patjens Lakes Loop

This fun lake loop takes you on a tour of the Patjens Lakes and Big Lake in the Mount Washington Wilderness.

Distance: 6.2-mile loop
Hiking time: 3–4 hours
Elevation gain: 400 feet
Trail surface: Dirt path
Best season: July through Oct
Other trail users: None
Canine compatibility: Dogs permitted

Fees and permits: A free wilderness permit is required from June 15 to October 15 and is available at the trailhead.
Schedule: Open all hours
Maps: USFS Deschutes National Forest
USGS maps: Clear Lake, OR; Mount Washington, OR

Finding the trailhead: *From Sisters:* Travel west on US 20 to the turnoff for Hoodoo Ski Bowl. Turn left (south) onto Big Lake Road and continue 4 miles to a dirt pullout and the trailhead on the right side of the road. *From Salem:* Follow OR 22 east 82 miles to the junction with US 20. Stay left on US 20 toward Sisters and continue 6 miles to the turnoff for Hoodoo Ski Bowl. Turn right (south) onto Big Lake Road and continue 4 miles to a dirt pullout and the trailhead on the right side of the road. GPS: N44 22.37' / W121 52.50'

The Hike

This hike offers nice views of the Three Sisters, Belknap Crater, and Mount Washington. At the trailhead, fill out a wilderness permit before you enter the Mount Washington Wilderness. Begin hiking on the Patjens Lake Trail 3395. The trail passes through a pine forest carpeted with clumps of bear grass and lupine. Early in the season, you'll pass small snowmelt ponds beginning at 0.8 mile. At 1.2 miles you'll

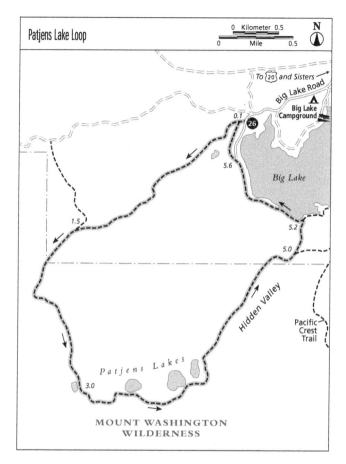

Patjens Lake Loop

0 Kilometer 0.5
0 Mile 0.5

N

To 20 and Sisters

Big Lake Road

Big Lake Campground

0.1

26

5.6

Big Lake

1.5

5.2

5.0

Hidden Valley

Pacific Crest Trail

Patjens Lakes

3.0

MOUNT WASHINGTON WILDERNESS

ford a small creek. At 1.5 miles, stay left and continue on the main trail as it begins climbing over a low pass.

As you ascend, you'll have views over the trees of the Three Sisters and Belknap Crater. At 3.0 miles you'll arrive at a small lake on the right. A side trail leads to the lake's edge. As you continue, you'll pass another lake on the left at 3.5 miles. A side trail heads down to the lake on the left. After 5.2 miles you'll arrive at scenic Big Lake. Big Lake covers approximately 225 acres and offers good fishing for kokanee, rainbow, and cutthroat trout. Enjoy the views of Hayrick Butte and the jagged summit of Mount Washington. At 6.1 miles you'll end the loop portion of the hike. Turn right and continue 0.1 mile back to the trailhead. If you want to explore this area more, you can set up camp at Big Lake Campground. Be armed with mosquito repellent on this hike.

Miles and Directions

0.0 Fill out a free wilderness permit at the trailhead and begin walking on the trail signed PATJENS LAKE TRAIL 3395.

0.1 Turn right at the trail fork to begin the loop.

1.2 Cross a small creek.

1.5 Turn left and ascend a small pass.

3.0 Pass a lake on the right. A side trail leads to the lake's edge.

3.5 Pass a lake on the left. A side trail leads to the lake's edge.

5.0 Turn left at the trail fork.

5.2 Arrive at Big Lake and stay to the left.

5.6 Turn left at the trail fork. The trail that heads right leads to Big Lake Campground.

6.1 End loop; turn right.

6.2 Arrive back at the trailhead.

Redmond

27 Alder Springs

This hidden gem is one of the best trails in the Crooked River National Grassland. It takes you into a dramatic canyon carved by Whychus Creek. Bubbling Whychus Creek is fed by several natural springs that you can view along the route. The trail parallels Whychus Creek and passes by some hidden camp spots shaded by towering ponderosa pine trees. The trail follows Whychus Creek until the turnaround point, where the creek joins up with the Deschutes River.

Distance: 7.4 miles out and back
Hiking time: 3-5 hours
Elevation gain: 950 feet
Trail surface: Dirt path
Best season: Apr through Nov
Other trail users: None

Canine compatibility: Dogs permitted
Fees and permits: None
Schedule: Open all hours
Maps: Crooked River National Grassland, BLM Prineville District
USGS map: Henkle Butte, OR

Finding the trailhead: From Redmond travel 6.5 miles north on US 97, passing through the small town of Terrebonne. On the north end of Terrebonne, turn left onto Lower Bridge Way. Travel 16.9 miles on Lower Bridge Way, then turn left onto Holmes Road. Go 2.2 miles on Holmes Road and turn right onto FR 6360 (a dirt doubletrack road). Go through the green gate and continue 4 miles; turn right where a sign indicates ALDER SPRINGS. Continue another 0.8 mile to the trailhead and parking area. GPS: N44 25.966' / W121 21.462'

The Hike

If you are seeking solitude with scenery and opportunities for swimming during the summer months, you will want

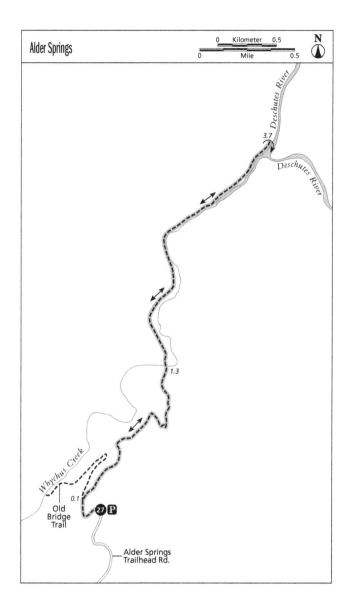

Alder Springs

0   Kilometer   0.5

0   Mile   0.5

N

Deschutes River

3.7

Deschutes River

1.3

Whychus Creek

0.1

Old
Bridge
Trail

27 P

Alder Springs
Trailhead Rd.

to check out this hike. It is in the Crooked River National Grassland and is enough off the beaten path that you will not see many other people. Use caution if you are hiking with your canine partner during the summer months. The canyon can be very hot, and the trail surface can heat up enough that it will burn the pads of your dog's feet. If you do want to hike on a hot day, be sure to bring foot protection for your dog.

You start hiking on the dirt path that descends into the Whychus Creek Canyon over the next 1.3 miles. You'll have nice views of the Central Cascade Mountains as well as the impressive Deschutes formation that exposes the multicolored layers of volcanic rock and eroded rock spires. You'll also see many of the natural springs that feed Whychus Creek bubbling out of the rocky ground. After 0.1 mile you will arrive at a signed trail junction for the Old Bridge Trail. If you want to explore this spur trail, turn left and follow the trail 0.3 mile downhill to the junction with Whychus Creek. After 1.3 miles you will arrive at Whychus Creek and a crossing. (Bring extra shoes for this crossing.) The creek is lined with shaded grassy banks and abundant greenery. After crossing the creek follow the dirt path as it parallels the creek for another 2.4 miles. Along the way you'll pass many hidden campsites shaded by towering ponderosa pines that make excellent places to spend the night (and have great swimming spots) if you plan on backpacking into the canyon. The trail's turnaround point is where the creek joins the Deschutes River. Giant boulders and towering ponderosas make the turnaround point a great place to take a break and enjoy views of the fast-flowing Deschutes River.

Miles and Directions

0.0 Start hiking on the dirt path.

0.1 The trail intersects with the signed OLD BRIDGE TRAIL, which goes left. (*Option:* For a side trip continue on this trail 0.3 mile downhill to its end at Whychus Creek.)

1.3 Arrive at Whychus Creek. Cross the creek and continue on the dirt path.

3.7 Arrive at the trail's turnaround point under towering ponderosa pine trees and large boulders next to the Deschutes River. Retrace your route back to your starting point.

7.4 Arrive back at the trailhead.

28 Smith Rock State Park

This scenic loop explores the volcanic landscapes of Smith Rock State Park. This world-class climbing area is packed with challenging multipitch routes, miles of hiking trails, and gorgeous scenery. This route takes you into a scenic river canyon carved by the Crooked River and then ascends to the top of Staender Ridge, where you'll have outstanding views of the Central Cascade peaks and the surrounding Central Oregon farmland and high desert. You will then descend back into the river canyon and have nice views of the Crooked River and the amazing rock spire called Monkey Face.

Distance: 7.8-mile loop
Hiking time: 3.5–4.5 hours
Elevation gain: 800 feet
Trail surface: Paved path, doubletrack road, and dirt path
Best season: Apr through Oct
Other trail users: Mountain bikers, horseback riders, and trail runners
Canine compatibility: Leashed dogs permitted. This trail is not recommended for dogs during July and Aug due to the extreme heat.

Fees and permits: A day-use permit is required and can be purchased at the self-pay station at the park. You can also purchase a day-use permit or an annual Oregon State Parks permit by credit card by calling (800) 551-6949.
Schedule: Dawn to dusk
Maps: Smith Rock Climbing and Trail Guide can be found at www.oregonstateparks.org.
USGS map: Redmond, OR

Finding the trailhead: From Redmond drive approximately 5 miles north on US 97 to the small town of Terrebonne. At the flashing yellow light, turn right onto B Avenue (this becomes Smith Rock Way after the first stop sign). Drive 3.3 miles northeast, following the signs to Smith Rock State Park. GPS: N44 21.894' / W121 08.287'

The Hike

Smith Rock is one of Central Oregon's most popular state parks. As you start the hike, you'll enjoy spectacular views of the park's colorful 400-foot-tall cliffs. These volcanic masterpieces started to take shape in the Miocene period, 17 to 19 million years ago, when hot steam and ash spewed from the ground. Traces of basalt can be found from the Newberry Volcano eruption 1.2 million years ago that formed Paulina and East Lakes. Since this volcanic activity the Crooked River has eroded the rock to form the columnar shapes that you see in the upper gorge today.

This 7.8-mile loop route begins from the main parking area and takes you past a shady picnic area with restrooms. You then begin a steep descent to the canyon floor. A maintained viewpoint and interpretive sign along the way is an excellent place to take photos and to learn more about the park's geologic history.

Please be aware that during the hot summer months of July and August this route is not recommended for canine companions because the ground can become very hot and burn your dog's feet. If you are hiking with your dog during the hot summer months, be sure you have foot protection for them. A cheap alternative to buying dog boots is to bring along a roll of Vetwrap, which is a stretchy gauze material that you can wrap your dog's paws with in the event of a foot injury. In addition, be aware that during this time you may see rattlesnakes.

Once you reach the canyon floor, you will cross the Crooked River on a wooden footbridge and then turn right onto the Wolf Tree Trail. This trail parallels the Crooked River and winds through the scenic river canyon that is surrounded by stunning rock spires. Along this stretch of the trail watch for Canada geese, whose striking white throat patch and black head and neck make them easy to spot. The geese feed on the riverside vegetation and are apt to honk in alarm as you approach. Also keep an eye out for river otters, which are sometimes seen along this stretch of the river.

After 1.4 miles you'll turn left and start climbing steeply uphill on the Burma Road Trail. The Burma Road Trail ascends steeply over the next 1.1 miles to the spectacular summit of Staender Ridge. Be sure to take a break and soak in the views of the Three Sisters, Broken Top, and other Central Cascade peaks as well as the amazing rock spires of Smith Rock. From the summit you will hook up with the Summit Loop Trail, which descends for a few miles along the northern edge of the park to the junction with the River Trail. Follow the River Trail as it parallels the Crooked River over the next 2.4 miles. Along the way there are some good swimming holes with small sandy beaches that are worth checking out. Finish the loop by crossing the wooden footbridge and making the short, steep climb back to your starting point.

Miles and Directions

- **0.0** From the parking area, follow the paved trail as it parallels the canyon rim.
- **0.2** Turn left onto the wide path that descends into the canyon. Go a short distance and turn right onto The Chute Trail.
- **0.4** Pass a drinking fountain and rest area on the right, then cross a wooden footbridge over the Crooked River. After crossing the bridge, turn right onto the Wolf Tree Trail.
- **1.4** At the trail junction turn left and start hiking uphill. After about 50 feet turn left onto the signed BURMA ROAD TRAIL. (*Note:* If you go right, the trail heads toward the Student

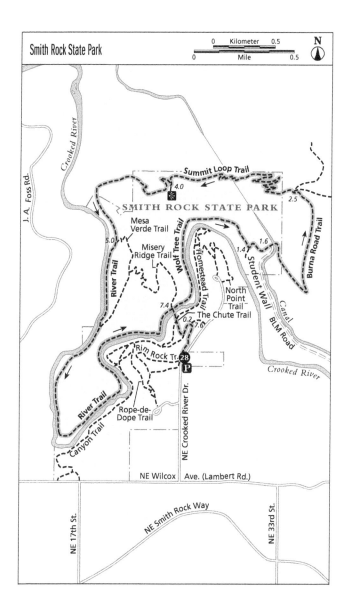

Kilometer

Mile

N

Crooked River

J. A. Foss Rd.

Summit Loop Trail

4.0

SMITH ROCK STATE PARK

2.5

Mesa
Verde Trail

5.0

Misery
Ridge Trail

Wolf Tree Trail

Homestead Trail

Burna Road Trail

1.6

1.4

Student Wall

River Trail

7.4

North
Point
Trail

The Chute Trail

0.2

7.6

Canal

BLM Road

Crooked River

Rim Rock Tr.

28

P

River Trail

Rope-de-
Dope Trail

Canyon Trail

NE Crooked River Dr.

NE Wilcox Ave. (Lambert Rd.)

NE 17th St.

NE Smith Rock Way

NE 33rd St.

Wall—a climbing area that is popular with beginning climbers.)

1.6 Turn left onto the signed BURMA ROAD TRAIL.

2.5 Arrive at the top of Staender Ridge. Take a break and soak in the gorgeous views. At the junction with the Summit Loop Trail, turn left and start descending.

4.0 Arrive at the junction with the signed SUMMIT LOOP VIEWPOINT. Go right and continue hiking on the Summit Loop Trail. After another 0.5 mile you'll have great views of Monkey Face—a stunning 350-foot rock with multiple climbing routes and a cave that mimics a monkey's mouth.

5.0 Arrive at a junction with the Mesa Verde Trail. Continue straight (right) and follow the River Trail as it parallels the Crooked River.

7.4 Turn right and cross the wooden footbridge. Follow the trail until it intersects with The Chute Trail. Turn left onto The Chute Trail and follow it until you reach the canyon rim.

7.6 Turn right onto the path that follows the canyon rim.

7.8 Arrive back at the trailhead.

29 Gray Butte

This route travels through a fragrant sage and juniper landscape of the Crooked River National Grasslands. At the trail's turnaround point, you'll have grand views of the Central Cascade Mountains.

Distance: 3.8 miles out and back

Hiking time: 2-3 hours

Elevation gain: 200 feet

Trail surface: Dirt path

Best season: Apr through Oct

Other trail users: Mountain bikers and horseback riders

Canine compatibility: Dogs permitted

Fees and permits: No fees or permits required

Schedule: Open all hours

Maps: Crooked River National Grassland map

USGS map: Gray Butte, OR

Finding the trailhead: From Redmond travel 5 miles north on US 97 to the small town of Terrebonne. At the flashing yellow light in Terrebonne, turn east onto B Avenue (after a short distance B Avenue becomes Smith Rock Way). Continue 4.9 miles on Smith Rock Way to Lone Pine Road. Turn left on Lone Pine Road and go 4.4 miles to FR 5710. Turn left onto FR 5710 (you'll pass Skull Hollow Campground on your left). Follow FR 5710 as it winds up Skull Hollow Canyon for 2.6 miles. Turn left onto FR 57. Continue 0.6 mile to a gravel pullout on the left side of the road. GPS: N44 23.974' / W121 5.891'

The Hike

The Gray Butte Trail skirts the southwest edge of Gray Butte and travels through open grassland filled with fragrant sagebrush and juniper trees. This prominent butte rises 5,108 feet above the Central Oregon high desert and is part of a

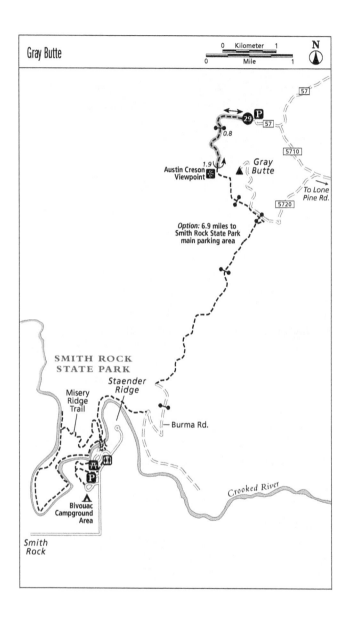

Gray Butte

0   Kilometer   1

0   Mile   1

N

57

P 29   57

0.8

1.9

Austin Creson
Viewpoint

Gray
Butte

5710

5720

To Lone
Pine Rd.

Option: 6.9 miles to
Smith Rock State Park
main parking area

SMITH ROCK
STATE PARK

Staender
Ridge

Misery
Ridge
Trail

Burma Rd.

Crooked River

Bivouac
Campground
Area

Smith
Rock

series of rounded buttes that provide a unique texture to the landscape. Gray Butte is part of the Crooked River National Grassland established in 1960. Although the grasslands are public property managed by the USDA Forest Service, large portions of the Crooked River National Grassland are open to range cattle from April through October.

After following the singletrack trail for 1.9 miles you'll arrive at a side trail on the right that leads to the Austin Creson Viewpoint. A memorial plaque for Austin Creson is located at this point and is dedicated to his hard work on planning the Gray Butte Trail. From the viewpoint you'll have spectacular views of the Three Sisters Mountains, Broken Top, Black Butte, and Mount Jefferson. After enjoying the views, retrace the route back to the trailhead.

If you are feeling ambitious, you can continue 6.9 miles on the Gray Butte Trail to Smith Rock State Park.

Miles and Directions

0.0 The singletrack trail starts on the northeast edge of Gray Butte. The trail climbs slowly as it rounds the north edge of the butte.

0.9 Go through a green metal gate and continue your stroll through this magnificent high-desert landscape.

1.9 Turn right onto a side trail that leads to the Austin Creson Viewpoint. After enjoying the views, retrace your route back to the trailhead. (***Option:*** Continue 6.9 miles to the Smith Rock State Park main parking area. You can leave a car at Smith Rock and complete this as a shuttle hike.)

3.8 Arrive back at the trailhead.

30 Rimrock Springs Natural Area

This easy hike takes you on a tour of the fragrant juniper and sagebrush landscape of the Rimrock Springs Natural Area. This wildlife area features a productive marsh where you can see geese, ducks, and other wildlife from two viewing platforms along the route. This hike also features interpretive signs in English and Spanish, and the first 0.5 mile of the trail is paved.

Distance: 1.7-mile loop
Hiking time: 1 hour
Elevation gain: 230 feet
Trail surface: Paved path and dirt path
Best season: Open year-round
Other trail users: None

Canine compatibility: Dogs permitted
Fees and permits: No fees or permits required
Schedule: Open all hours
Maps: Crooked River National Grassland map
USGS map: Gray Butte, OR

Finding the trailhead: *From Redmond:* Drive 5 miles north on US 97 to the small town of Terrebonne. At the flashing yellow light, turn right onto B Avenue (Smith Rock Way). Go 4.7 miles and turn left (north) onto Lone Pine Road. Continue 7.2 miles to the intersection with US 26. Turn left onto US 26 and go 4.4 miles to the parking area signed RIMROCK SPRINGS WILDLIFE MANAGEMENT AREA, located on the right side of the highway. *From Madras:* Drive south on US 97 for about 2 miles to a sign that indicates PRINEVILLE/ MITCHELL/ JOHN DAY. Turn left (east) onto US 26. Travel 8.5 miles to a parking area signed RIMROCK SPRINGS WILDLIFE MANAGEMENT AREA located on the left side of the highway. GPS: N44 29.728' / W121 03.361'

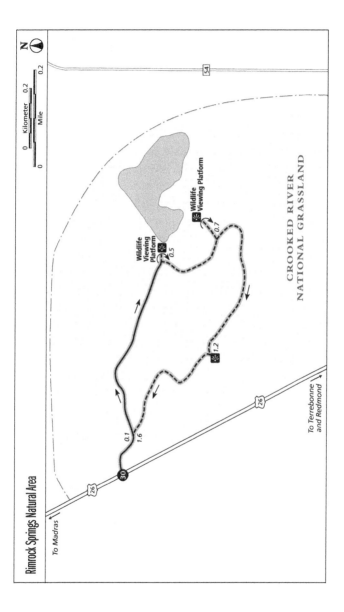

Rimrock Springs Natural Area

To Madras

To Terrebonne
and Redmond

CROOKED RIVER
NATIONAL GRASSLAND

Wildlife Viewing Platform

Wildlife
Viewing
Platform

N

Kilometer   0   0.2

Mile   0   0.2

The Hike

This short hike travels through a sagebrush and juniper landscape in the Rimrock Springs Natural Area located in the Crooked River National Grassland.

You'll start the hike by walking on a paved path for 0.5 mile to a side trail that leads to a wooden viewing platform. From the platform you'll have nice views of a productive cattail marsh. Look for ducks, geese, and raptors.

After enjoying the view, continue on the main trail. In the spring months look for the striking lupine wildflower, which has purple-bluish blossoms and silvery green leaves. You may also see jackrabbits hopping through the sagebrush and small groups of quail. At 0.7 mile turn left onto a side trail that leads to another viewing platform. Return to the main trail as it climbs to the top of a small rise and takes you next to some jumbled lava outcroppings. At 1.2 miles turn left at a signed viewpoint where you have views of a wide valley and the Three Sisters Mountains with Mount Bachelor as a backdrop. After 1.6 miles the loop portion of the trail ends, and you'll follow the paved path back to the trailhead.

Miles and Directions

0.0 Start hiking on the paved path adjacent to the parking area.

0.1 The trail forks; go left.

0.5 Arrive at a trail junction (the paved path ends). Turn left and walk on a side trail to a viewing platform. Enjoy the views of the marsh and then return to the main trail. Back at the main trail, turn left and continue on the signed loop trail.

0.7 Turn left onto a side trail that leads to another viewing platform. After enjoying the views, return to the main trail and turn left to continue the loop.

1.2 Turn left at the signed viewpoint. Enjoy views of the Three Sisters and Mount Bachelor. After soaking in the views, return to the main loop trail and turn left.

1.6 The loop trail ends. Turn left onto the paved path.

1.7 Arrive back at the trailhead.

Madras

31 Tam-a-lau Loop

This loop trail takes you more than 550 feet to the top of a high peninsula above Lake Billy Chinook in Cove Palisades State Park. From there you have far-reaching views of the vast reservoir below and the snowcapped Central Cascade peaks, including Mount Hood, Mount Jefferson, Broken Top, Mount Bachelor, and the Three Sisters. The Crooked, Deschutes, and Metolius Rivers feed this giant lake, which is popular with boaters.

Distance: 6.8-mile loop
Hiking time: 3.5–4.5 hours
Elevation gain: 600 feet
Trail surface: Paved path, steps, dirt path
Best season: Sept through June. This hike can be very hot during July and Aug.
Other trail users: None
Canine compatibility: Leashed dogs permitted

Fees and permits: A day-use permit is required. You can purchase a day-use permit at the park or purchase an annual Oregon State Parks permit by credit card by calling (800) 551-6949.
Schedule: Dawn to dusk
Maps: Tam-a-lau Hiking Trail and Map available at www.oregon stateparks.org.
USGS map: The Dalles, OR

Finding the trailhead: *From Redmond:* Travel 19 miles north on US 97 to a turnoff for Cove Palisades State Park and Culver/Round Butte Dam. Turn left (west) onto the Culver Highway and follow the state park signs for 6 miles to the park entrance. Follow the entrance road down into the canyon to a road junction. At the bottom of the canyon, turn left toward Deschutes Campground and day-use areas. Continue 3.7 miles to another road junction. Drive past the campground entrance and continue 0.25 mile to the signed TAM-A-LAU PARKING AREA. *From Madras:* Follow US 97 south and then follow signs approximately 15 miles southwest to the park. Once you reach the park entrance, follow the directions described above. GPS: N44 3.461' / W121 17.334'

The Hike

This high desert hike gives you incredible views from the high rocky plateau called The Peninsula. The route climbs at a steady pace for a little over a mile to the top of a long, flat plateau. The hillside is blanketed with bunchgrass, yellow balsamroot, and purple lupine mixed with fragrant rabbitbrush and sagebrush.

After 1.6 miles you'll start the loop section of the hike, located on the top of The Peninsula. This plateau is made up of rock and sediment that were deposited by the Deschutes River over thousands of years. The sediment and rock are mixed with layers of basalt, a result of massive lava flows that covered this area from different eruptions of Cascade volcanoes. The lava flows filled the three river canyons carved by the Deschutes, Metolius, and Crooked Rivers, water sources for Lake Billy Chinook. Over thousands of years the rivers carved away the rock layers to produce the magnificent canyons that are present here today.

After 2.7 miles you'll arrive at a dramatic viewpoint and a great place to take a break and eat lunch. After 5.2 miles you'll end the loop and descend on the same route back to your starting point.

Avoid this hike during July and August when temperatures can hover in the 90s. If you're visiting during those months, explore the trail in the early morning when it is cooler, and be sure to bring plenty of water.

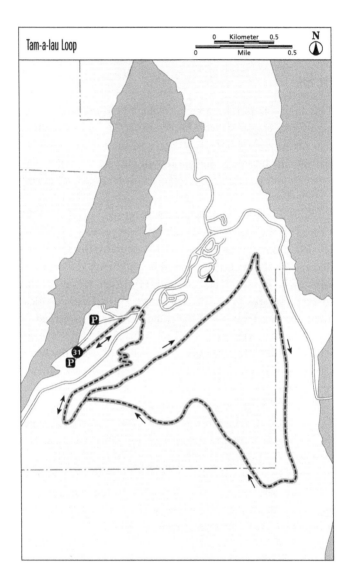

Tam-a-lau Loop

Miles and Directions

0.0 Start hiking toward the entrance to the parking area. On the left side of the road, at the brown hiker symbol, turn onto a hiking trail that parallels the road.

0.1 Cross a paved road and walk through an opening in a fence around Deschutes Campground.

0.5 Turn right onto a dirt path adjacent to a large interpretive sign. Over the next 1.1 miles, the trail ascends steeply to a high plateau above the lake.

1.4 Turn left onto a wide doubletrack road.

1.6 Turn left and begin the loop portion of the hike. Follow the dirt path as it parallels the edge of the rimrock and offers outstanding views of the lake canyon and the Central Cascade peaks.

2.7 Arrive at the tip of The Peninsula, which serves as a good lunch spot.

5.2 The loop portion of the hike ends. Descend on the same route back to your starting point.

6.8 Arrive back at the parking area.

Prineville

32 Chimney Rock

This route takes you to the base of Chimney Rock—a prominent formation located high above the Crooked River. Along the way, you'll walk through a high-desert ecosystem of sage and juniper and enjoy views of the Crooked River Canyon and Cascade Mountains.

Distance: 2.8 miles out and back
Hiking time: 1–1.5 hours
Elevation gain: 500 feet
Trail surface: Dirt path
Best season: Open year-round
Other trail users: None

Canine compatibility: Dogs permitted
Fees and permits: No fees or permits required
Schedule: Open all hours
Maps: BLM Prineville Reservoir Recreation Area
USGS map: Stearns Butte, OR

Finding the trailhead: From US 26 in Prineville, turn south onto Main Street (OR 27). Continue south for 17.1 miles to a gravel parking area on the left side of the road marked RIM TRAIL. The trailhead is located across from the Chimney Rock Recreation Area. GPS: N44 23.699' / W120 37.416'

The Hike

If you're seeking solitude, you'll enjoy this hike that climbs to the base of Chimney Rock and provides nice views of Crooked River Canyon and the Central Cascade Mountains. From the trailhead you'll follow a series of switchbacks up a grass- and sage-covered hillside. With each step, the views of the river canyon become more dramatic.

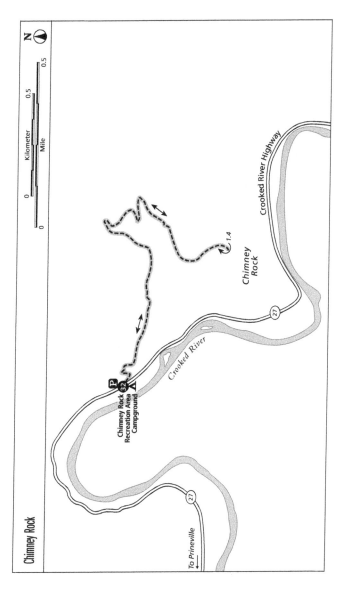

Chimney Rock

As the trail climbs higher, you'll pass some twisted and gnarled juniper trees. Their stunted growth hides their age—some of the trees here are more than a century old. After 1.4 miles you'll arrive at the dramatic spire of Chimney Rock. Enjoy the views, and then retrace your route back to the trailhead.

Miles and Directions

0.0 Start hiking on the signed dirt path.

1.0 Pass a rest bench.

1.4 Arrive at the base of Chimney Rock (your turnaround point). Retrace the route back to the trailhead.

2.8 Arrive back at the trailhead.

33 Steins Pillar

This route takes you through a towering ponderosa pine forest to the base of Steins Pillar—a dramatic rock tower that is a definitive landmark in this area. The route also offers glimpses of the Central Cascade Mountains and the surrounding Ochoco Mountains. This hike offers solitude and scenery and is a great escape to an uncrowded part of Central Oregon.

Distance: 4.2 miles out and back
Hiking time: 2–3 hours
Elevation gain: 700 feet
Trail surface: Dirt path
Best season: Open year-round
Other trail users: None
Canine compatibility: Dogs permitted

Fees and permits: No fees or permits required
Schedule: Open all hours
Maps: USFS Ochoco National Forest
USGS map: Salt Butte, OR; Steins Pillar, OR

Finding the trailhead: Travel 9.1 miles east of Prineville on US 26. Turn left (north) onto Mill Creek Road (FR 33). Travel 6.7 miles on Mill Creek Road (the road becomes gravel after 5.2 miles) to the junction with FR 500. Turn right onto FR 500 and continue 2.1 miles to the trailhead on the left side of the road. GPS: N44 23.699' / W120 37.416'

The Hike

Steins Pillar is a fascinating rock formation located in the heart of the Ochoco National Forest in the Ochoco Mountains. The 350-foot pillar is an important geologic remnant of the area's rich volcanic history. It is thought that this pillar was named after Major Enoch Steen of the US Army. In 1860 he was in charge of a raid against the Snake Indians, and he camped in the Mill Creek Valley not far from Steins Pillar.

Nearly 50 million years ago, this was volcano land. Eruptions layered the area in volcanic tuff, andesite, and ash. The Clarno and John Day Formations, world famous for their many fossils, were created because of these eruptions. James Condon, a young Congregational minister and naturalist, first discovered fossils in the area in the 1860s. His first find was an ancient tortoise shell in Picture Gorge in the John Day Valley. Over the next several years, Condon and others uncovered many more plant and animal fossils—the precursor to research and cataloging of hundreds of specimens in the area over the next century. Fossils that have been discovered here include amynodonts and brontotheres of the Clarno Formation period (37 to 54 million years ago) and dogs, cats, camels, oreodonts, swine, rhinoceroses, and rodents of the John Day Formation period (20 to 39 million years ago).

A great way to get a feel for the geologic history of the area is by hiking the moderate 2.1-mile trail to the base of Steins Pillar. The trail starts out fairly flat and travels through a dry, open forest of ponderosa pine and Douglas fir and then transitions into an open, rocky landscape filled with sagebrush and western juniper trees. The small, fragrant, bluish berries of the juniper are a favorite food of small birds and mammals. In spring and summer, wildflowers are scattered along the trail—bright red Indian paintbrush, bluish-purple lupine, and bright yellow mule's ears are just a few of the varieties you'll see.

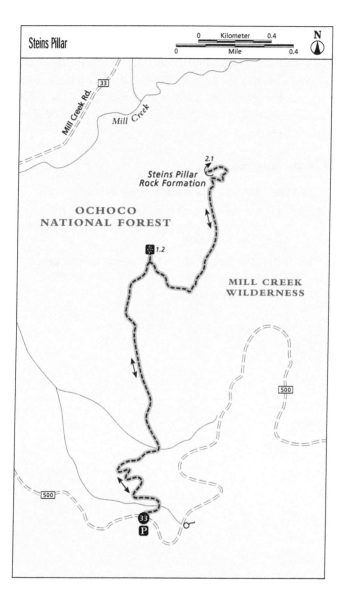

At 1.2 miles you'll pass a signed junction with a side trail that goes about 50 feet to a viewpoint. After 2.1 miles you'll reach the base of Steins Pillar, which rises prominently above the Mill Creek Valley. At the pillar's base look up to see why rock climbers find it such a tempting challenge. (The pillar was first climbed in 1950.) Admire the towering rock spire and then return on the same route.

Miles and Directions

0.0 Start on the dirt track next to a STEINS PILLAR TRAIL sign.

1.2 Turn left at the signed viewpoint. Go about 50 feet and admire the mountain views and then return to the main trail and turn left to continue.

2.1 Arrive at the base of 350-foot Steins Pillar and your turn-around point. Retrace the route back to the trailhead.

4.2 Arrive back at the trailhead.

34 Mill Creek Wilderness

This route follows Mill Creek and crosses it many times over 2.7 miles where you'll have opportunities to view a variety of wildlife and admire seasonal wildflowers. Be sure to bring sandals or other waterproof shoes for the many creek crossings. The optional remaining portion of the trail traverses a ponderosa pine forest interspersed with grassy meadows before arriving at the base of Twin Pillars, the eroded remnant of a volcano that erupted 40 to 50 million years ago.

Distance: 5.4 miles out and back (with a longer 10.5-mile round trip option that takes you to the base of Twin Pillars)

Hiking time: 3–6 hours (depending on how far you decide to hike)

Elevation gain: 200 feet to the 2.7-mile mark or 600 feet to the base of Twin Pillars

Trail surface: Dirt path and water crossings

Best season: June through Oct

Other trail users: Horseback riders

Canine compatibility: Dogs permitted

Fees and permits: No fees or permits required

Schedule: Open all hours

Maps: USFS Ochoco National Forest

USGS map: Steins Pillar, OR

Finding the trailhead: From Prineville drive 9.1 miles east on US 26 to Mill Creek Road (FR 33). Turn left (north) and travel 10.6 miles to a fork in the road. Turn right at the WILDCAT CAMPGROUND sign. Drive 0.1 mile and turn right into a gravel parking area at the trailhead. Wildcat Campground is another 0.3 mile past the parking area. GPS: N44 26.469' / W120 34.568'

The Hike

Located in the 17,000-acre Mill Creek Wilderness of the Ochoco National Forest, this route takes you on a trek along bubbling Mill Creek, passing through a forest of ponderosa pine, grand fir, and Douglas fir.

The trail begins with a series of creek crossings, so be sure to bring an old pair of tennis shoes or sandals to wear in the water. As you walk along the creek, you'll hear the cries of kingfishers protesting your presence on their home turf. Other birds in the area include pileated woodpeckers, wild turkeys, and northern goshawks. Pileated woodpeckers are the largest species of woodpecker and can be identified by their prominent red crests, black feathers, and white undersides. Northern goshawks, which weigh between 6 and 8 pounds and live up to ten years, have slate-gray feathers and bright orange-red eyes outlined in white. You'll most likely see them weaving in and out of the woodlands with great speed and finesse as they hunt for small birds and mammals. You may hear the distinctive "ca-ca-ca" hunting cry of a northern goshawk if you don't first see it. Other wildlife in this pristine wilderness area include Rocky Mountain elk, mule deer, bobcats, cougars, and black bears.

As you continue on the trail, you'll pass green meadows of daisies, delicate purple aster, crimson penstemon, and bright purple thistle. Tall stocks of woolly mullein with their bright bunches of yellow flowers are also common. Shimmering green aspen trees grow in clusters along the banks of the creek, and cutthroat trout hang out in shady rock pools.

After 2.7 miles you'll arrive at your turnaround point at a log bridge. From here you have the option of climbing a series of long and winding switchbacks for 2.6 miles to the base of the 200-foot-tall Twin Pillars rock formation.

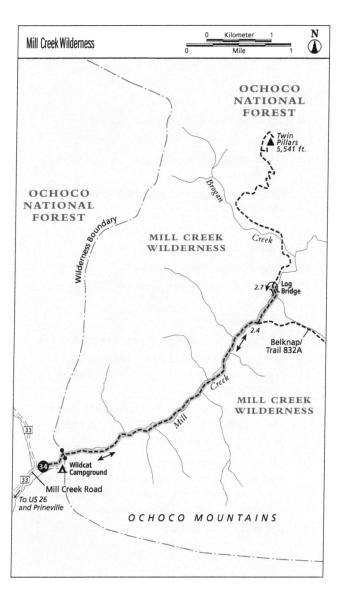

If you want to stay and explore this area more, pitch your tent at Wildcat Campground. The camping area is located just 0.3-mile northeast of the trailhead.

Miles and Directions

0.0 Start hiking on the signed TWIN PILLARS TRAIL 380.

0.1 Cross Mill Creek Road (FR 33) and continue straight.

0.2 Proceed through a green metal gate and enter the Mill Creek Wilderness.

0.3 Wade across Mill Creek. After the creek crossing the trail forks. Turn left.

0.8 Cross the creek.

0.9 Cross the creek.

1.1 Navigate another stream crossing.

1.2 Cross the creek. Proceed approximately 100 yards and cross again.

1.5 Cross the creek.

2.1 The trail forks. Turn left and continue along the main trail.

2.2 Arrive at another stream crossing. Logs are in place to help you cross. Walk another 50 yards and cross the stream again.

2.4 Cross the creek and arrive at a trail junction. Continue straight (left). (*Note:* Belknap Trail 832A goes right.)

2.5 Pass a sign on the left that reads TWIN PILLARS 2 MILES.

2.7 Arrive at a log bridge (your turnaround point). Retrace your route back to the trailhead. (***Option:*** If you want to continue to the base of Twin Pillars, continue ascending 2.6 miles to the base of this 200-foot-tall rock formation.)

5.4 Arrive back at the trailhead.

35 Painted Hills Unit–John Day Fossil Beds National Monument

The short hikes in the Painted Hills Unit of the John Day Fossil Beds National Monument provide a close-up look at the area's beautiful color-splashed hills and fascinating fossil beds. The Painted Hills Overlook Trail is a 1.0-mile out-and-back trail that takes you to the top of an overlook with views of the colorful surrounding hills. If you want more of an adventure, trek 1.5 miles to the top of Carroll Rim, where you'll have a sweeping view of the painted hills and surrounding high-desert country. If you want to see one of these hills up close, stroll the quarter-mile Painted Cove Trail. To view fossils of plants that dominated this area 33 million years ago, walk the Leaf Hill Trail. You can also take a short jaunt on the 0.4-mile Red Scar Knoll (Red Hill) Trail where you can view the striking yellow and red clay that makes up this unique landscape. It's possible to complete all four of the established trails in just a day.

Distance:
A. Carroll Rim Trail: 1.5 miles out and back
B. Painted Hills Overlook Trail: 1.0 mile out and back
C. Painted Cove Trail: 0.25-mile loop
D. Leaf Hill Trail: 0.25-mile loop
E. Red Scar Knoll (Red Hill) Trail: 0.4 mile out and back

Hiking time: Varies depending on the trail(s) selected
Elevation gain: Carroll Rim Trail: 400 feet; Painted Hills Overlook Trail: 100 feet
Trail surface: Dirt path
Best season: Open year-round
Other trail users: None
Canine compatibility: Leashed dogs permitted

Fees and permits: No fees or permits required

Schedule: Open dawn to dusk

Maps: Painted Hills Trail Map

USGS map: Painted Hills, OR

Finding the trailhead: From Prineville travel 45.2 miles east on US 26 to the junction with Burnt Ranch Road where a sign indicates JOHN DAY FOSSIL BEDS NATIONAL MONUMENT—PAINTED HILLS UNIT. Turn left (north) and go 5.7 miles. Turn left onto Bear Creek Road and proceed 0.9 mile to the turnoff for the Carroll Rim Trailhead. Turn left and then take an immediate right into the gravel parking area on the right. The Carroll Rim Trail begins on the opposite side of the road from the parking area. The 0.5-mile out-and-back Painted Hills Overlook Trail can also be accessed from this parking area. Follow the road signs to reach the Painted Cove Trail, Leaf Hill Trail, and Red Scar Knoll (Red Hill) Trail. GPS: N44 39.25' / W120 15.11'

The Hike

The Painted Hills Unit of the John Day Fossil Beds National Monument has several hikes offering glimpses of the area's rich geologic history. The hikes are easy to moderately difficult, and each provides a different perspective on the area's unique formations.

The most striking feature you'll notice are the round, multihued hills of colorful clay stone. Thirty million years ago, layers of ash were deposited in this area from volcanoes erupting to the west. Over millions of years, the forces of nature have carved and shaped the hills that you see today. Different elements such as aluminum, silicon, iron, magnesium, manganese, sodium, calcium, and titanium have combined to produce minerals that have unique properties and colors.

To get a bird's-eye view of the hills, take a short jaunt on the 1.0-mile out-and-back Painted Hills Overlook Trail,

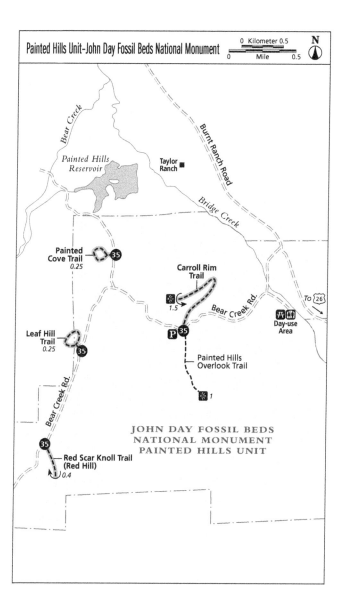

Painted Hills Unit–John Day Fossil Beds National Monument

0   Kilometer   0.5

0   Mile   0.5

N

Bear Creek

Painted Hills Reservoir

Taylor Ranch

Burnt Ranch Road

Bridge Creek

Painted Cove Trail
0.25
35

Leaf Hill Trail
0.25
35

Bear Creek Rd.

Carroll Rim Trail
1.5

Bear Creek Rd.

35
P

Painted Hills Overlook Trail
1

Day-use Area

To 26

JOHN DAY FOSSIL BEDS
NATIONAL MONUMENT
PAINTED HILLS UNIT

35
Red Scar Knoll Trail
(Red Hill)
0.4

which takes you up a gentle ridge and includes several view-points along the way. If you want a close-up view of one of these unique painted hills, take a walk on the 0.25-mile Painted Cove Trail loop. A brochure and corresponding trail markers offer an in-depth look at these geologic formations. For instance, the colors of the hills change with the weather. When it rains, the clay absorbs water, causing more light reflection and changing the color of the hills from red to pink and from light brown to yellow-gold. As the hills dry out, the soil contracts, causing surface cracking that diffuses the light and deepens the color of the hills. The purple layer in the hill is the weathered remains of a rhyolite lava flow. Other colored bands in the hillside are due to differences in mineral content and weathering. Plants can't grow on the painted hills because the clay is so dense that moisture can't penetrate the surface. Also, the clay soil is nutritionally poor.

Another distinguishing landmark of the Painted Hills Unit is Carroll Rim, a high ridge consisting of John Day ignimbrite, better known as "welded tuff." More than 28 million years ago, a volcano to the west erupted and hurled hot ash, debris, and gases into the air, which then landed and cooled to form a glasslike layer. To reach the top of this landmark and excellent views of the surrounding hills and valleys, hike the 1.5-mile out-and-back Carroll Rim Trail. From the top you'll be able to see Sutton Mountain, which rises prominently to the east.

For fossils, check out the 0.25-mile-long Leaf Hill Trail and its collection of ancient plants. The trail circles a small hill of loose shale deposits. While at first the hill seems somewhat unremarkable, a closer look reveals insights into the plants that once dominated here. The shales present in this hill were formed about 33 million years ago from lake-deposited volcanic ash. Fossils of thirty-five species of plants can be found at Laurel Hill, with alder, beech, maple, and the extinct hornbeam most prevalent. Other specimens include elm, rose, oak, grape, fern, redwood, and pine. Scientists have analyzed these plant fossils and concluded that this group of plants closely resembles two types of modern forests found in China—the mixed northern hardwood forest and the mixed mesophytic forest. Comparing the mix of plant species with these two modern forests indicates that in the past this area had a much higher rainfall content (up to 40 inches annually), milder temperatures, and a warmer climate than found here today. (Today the area receives about 12 to 15 inches of rain a year and experiences more extreme temperature variations.) In addition, the vegetation that grows here today is made up of high–desert–type plants—juniper, sagebrush, and grasses.

The 0.4-mile Red Scar Knoll (Red Hill) Trail gives you another interesting perspective of the striking yellow and red clay that makes up this unique landscape.

Miles and Directions

A. Carroll Rim Trail: A 1.5-mile out-and-back trek to the top of Carroll Rim that offers sweeping views of the surrounding hills and valleys.

B. Painted Hills Overlook Trail: A 1.0-mile out-and-back path with a panoramic view of the Painted Hills.

C. Painted Cove Trail: This 0.25-mile loop circles a painted hill and gives you a close-up look at the unique properties of these interesting geologic formations.

D. Leaf Hill Trail: This 0.25-mile loop circles a hill where ancient plant fossils are abundant.

E. Red Scar Knoll (Red Hill) Trail: This 0.4-mile out-and-back trail climbs a small hill to striking bright yellow and red clay.

About the Author

Lizann Dunegan is a freelance writer and photographer who specializes in writing outdoor guidebooks and travel articles about the Northwest. Her other books include *Best Hikes Near Bend, Best Easy Day Hikes Portland, Hiking Oregon, Best Bike Rides Portland*, and *Road Biking Oregon*.

Lizann enjoys exploring the trails in Oregon with her canine partners Zane and Zepplin. Lizann also enjoys backpacking, horseback riding, running, and mountain biking.

THE TEN ESSENTIALS OF HIKING

American Hiking Society

Whether you plan to be gone for a couple of hours or several months, make sure to pack these items. Become familiar with these items and know how to use them.

Find other helpful resources at AmericanHiking.org/hiking-resources

1. Appropriate Footwear

6. Safety Items (light, fire, and a whistle)

2. Navigation

7. First Aid Kit

3. Water (and a way to purify it)

8. Knife or Multi-Tool

4. Food

9. Sun Protection

5. Rain Gear & Dry-Fast Layers

10. Shelter

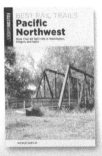